Anniversary History of
John "Hannes" Miller, Sr.

(ca 1730-1798)

On the 200th anniversary of
his death at his farm "Miller's Choice"
in the Glades near Berlin, Pennsylvania

by
J. Virgil Miller

Anniversary History of the Family of John "Hannes" Miller, Sr.
(ca1730-1798)

Copyright © 1998
by
Masthof Press
220 Mill Road
Morgantown, PA 19543

Cover

J. Virgil Miller (author) and Thomas Maust at the farm cemetery where John Miller, Sr., and his wife, Magdalena (?Lehman) are buried. The marker says "M1817M" meaning "Magdalena Miller died in 1817."

Library of Congress Number: 98-67102
International Standard Book Number: 1-883294-74-6

Published 1998 by
Masthof Press
220 Mill Road
Morgantown, PA 19543-9701

Table of Contents

Preface v

Acknowledgements vii

Dedication ix

The Family of John Miller, Sr. 1

Last Years of Hannes or John Miller, Sr. 9

Location of the Miller Homesteads 11

Locating the John Miller, Sr., Homestead in Brothers Valley in the Glades ... 19

Ancestry of John Miller, Sr., As Reconstructed From the Sources 23

I. The Family of Barbara Miller and Jacob Hochstetler,
   Oldest Child of John Miller, Sr. 29

II. The Family of John Miller, Jr., and Freny Yoder 33

III. The Family of Jacob Miller and Anna Stutzman 39

IV. The Family of Peter Miller and Mary Stutzman 45

V. The Family of Catherine Miller and Jacob Kauffman 51

VI. The Family of "Glades" Christian Miller and Freny (?Blough) 57

VII. The Family of Joseph Miller and 1) Barbara Speicher and
   2) Barbara Bontrager 65

VIII. The Family of Maria Miller and John Schrock, Jr. 69

IX. The Family of Freny Miller and Christian Speicher, Jr. 73

X. The Family of (?Susanna) Miller and Christian Mishler 77

XI. The Family of Elizabeth Miller and Joseph Speicher 82

Other Amish-Mennonite Families in Europe and America 86

Some Statistics and Interesting Facts About the Family of
    John Miller, Sr. 91

How You and I Are Descended From John Miller, Sr. 95

Appendix No. I: Family of John Miller 96

Appendix No. II: The Glades Amish of Brothersvalley 105

Appendix No. III: A Trip to the Glades:
    Reflections on the Homestead—June 18, 1996 116

Index 120

Preface

The name John Miller is one of the most common in the United States, and if you include both the English- and German-speaking worlds, it becomes even more numerous. In German its equivalent is Johannes Müller or just Hannes or Hans, which can be found in Germany proper, Switzerland, Alsace, or any other place where a form of German is spoken. In the index to the *Pennsylvania German Pioneers* by Ralph Strassburger and William Hinke, there are perhaps 200 persons listed with a form of Johannes Müller, who came to Pennsylvania between 1727 and 1808. Some of these names are a form beginning with Hans, such as Hans Jacob, Johann Georg, or Johannes Heinrich. Others are simply written Hans, and quite often with an X indicating that he was illiterate, a not uncommon occurrence in Europe during that period.

In the face of that evidence, how can we hope to find the right John Miller or Johannes Müller? Fortunately there are other clues that help to narrow the gap between the known and unknown. First, John Miller, Sr., was an Amish-Mennonite, called Anabaptist or *Wiedertaüfer* in Europe. His name was Johannes Müller to begin with, though he was called Hannes. We know the family names of other families related to or intermarried with his family. We also know the names of other Miller or Müller families that we are reasonably sure are related to his. It is also known that the group of families he was related to and associated with came from Switzerland and were expelled as religious dissidents from Canton Bern in the later 1600s or early 1700s. We know the places to which they fled and the routes they took.

Various archives and census records contain valuable lists of Anabaptist families. In the United States we have ship lists, early tax lists, and census records beginning in 1790. Unfortunately, the Anabaptists kept few records. They were not on the official rolls of the state churches in Europe unless a notation was made that the family was Anabaptist and refused to baptize their infants, or lists of dissidents were sent to the authorities, which found their way into the state archives.

If they were so fortunate (or unfortunate) to be occupied by the French after their revolution, as they were in Alsace and parts of Germany, all persons were listed in civil records, including dissidents, but that was only after 1790, and many of these people were in America by then. Even in America, while the Lutherans, Reformed, and Catholic churches kept records of births, marriages, and deaths, the Amish and Mennonite churches kept only scattered records, occasionally in a family Bible or a ledger. The family historian is still obliged to go to the civil records which exist; however, even these records are not complete.

Much of the research on this family has had of necessity to be done inductively. In the absence of concrete data, many facts have had to be deduced from the identity of persons listed next to them or in the same family, coordinated with geographical and chronological data. Reliance has been on published family histories, but always with a question as to the degree of accuracy. It was related to verifying documents if possible; however, some questionable folklore has been omitted. There is a lot of folklore which begins, "The story is told," or "So the story goes," and then some added variations. I'll leave that to the folklorists. On the other hand, I want to present real people as I think they were, without the embellishment of character or aura of sanctity we are tempted to give our ancestors.

Hopefully, it will show the Millers as they were, noting what is missing and what might yet be discovered.

Acknowledgements

I would like to acknowledge the help which I have had in doing this research. I have tried to use all the books, articles, and documents which are available on this subject. If there are others, it means that I have not known about them or I was not able to get access to them. This is especially true of materials in archives in Europe, where I have taken many notes over a period of many years, some in times when photocopies were not available. In most cases making photocopies of all the sources would have been physically impossible. I have relied on my own notes, mostly done in longhand and then typed, making the possibility of error fairly great.

In some cases I have had to rely on the notes of others who have shared their research with me. I would like especially to thank Erwin Hochstättler of Cologne, Germany, who probed many of the sources in Europe, and Hermann Guth of Saarbrücken, Germany, who gave me access to his notes even before the publication of his book *Amish-Mennonites in Germany,* published by Masthof Press in 1995.

In most cases I have indicated where the source can be found, rather than the person who found it. I have not given detailed references such as archive numbers, etc., because I do not have them, or because I got them with no detailed number. In most cases it should provide the serious researcher with clues about where further information might be obtained.

I have used family histories, especially the two large histories of the Hochstetler family (*DJH* and *DBH*), always with a critical eye because at the present time some items may be better known than previously, and all such compilations necessarily have some errata. On the other hand, I praise the Hochstetler-Stutzman volumes as the most extensive and accurate genealogy of Amish-Mennonite families available. Working for the past ten years as contributing editor of the *Hochstetler Newsletter*, however, has shown me that the work has its errors and omissions, such as the Miller family summary in the Appendix (also in this book) *DJH*-9146, by Moses B. Miller.

I also acknowledge the tremendous help I received from the work of Hugh Gingerich and Rachel Kreider, *Amish and Amish-Mennonite Genealogies*, 1986, published by Pequea Publishers, Gordonville, Pennsylvania. I have been helped in filling many of the missing branches of the Miller family by the above work. I am ever grateful to *AAMG* for sorting out especially the various Christian Millers and the two Jacob Kauffmans who were married to a Catherine Miller and lived in the same township at approximately the same time. But I also appreciate the general outline and their indexing system.

If I seem to be criticizing *AAMG* at times, I do it after examining the sources; the Miller family especially needs revision. Their system of ?? is good, but in this case they should have been put at more places. I have also indulged in considerable theorizing, but hopefully with some logic to back it up. I have not used question marks, but when I say probably, perhaps, and it might be, I mean that I am not sure. So the family historian has to do a certain amount of intelligent guessing and theorizing. I hope my original premises are correct.

History is not all facts. It may be a discussion of what could be, hopefully not what I would like it to be. We have to use imagination to describe how it might have been in other times, but I don't have the right to say this is what he said, or this is how it was, without some source to back it up. I am sure the authors of *AAMG* also wish to set the record straight. They have already done so for numerous family lines where they have corrected faulty information or added information to make it more complete.

I hope those who see this book will do the same for me.

- J. Virgil Miller
3217 Vinson Avenue
Sarasota, FL 34232

Dedication

I dedicate this history to many people, but especially to the Miller family of which I am a part; to the late Paul Hostetler of Mt. Carmel, Connecticut, who can be credited with "discovering" the John Miller, Sr., farm in modern times; to the late Evan Miller, who first showed me around Somerset County; to his daughter Marie and her husband, Paul Yoder, of the Benedict Miller clan, who introduced me to many more homesteads and cemeteries; to Marie's Aunt Kate, who was always willing, while she could, to share her findings; to the Maust family, who have graciously welcomed us in our visits to the homestead.

Finally, to my wife Susan, who endured many winding and hilly country roads to look for homesteads and clues to our family background, both in Europe and America. These last few months she painstakingly proofread the whole manuscript and made helpful suggestions.

In celebration of our continuing family, I would like especially to dedicate it to my three daughters and their families.

- J. Virgil Miller

The Family of John Miller, Sr.

John or Hannes Miller was an Amish-Mennonite immigrant to Pennsylvania in the 1700s. He has been variously called Indian John, Wounded John, and even Crippled John by family historians, from a single incident in his life in which he is said to have been wounded as the Hochstetler family was being taken into captivity by the Indians in 1757.[1] Moses B. Miller has an account of the John Miller family in the Hochstetler history; he was a great-grandson of John Miller. William F. Hochstetler, the author of the historical part of the genealogy, does not give a written source for the incident about being wounded. This may be a tradition in the family or from members of the community. There is no documentary evidence for the various nicknames, so we don't know if they arose from the account in the Hochstetler history or from stories told by descendants.

In light of that, where do we start? Moses B. Miller's account is likely the most reliable. The Millers and Hochstetlers lived in the Northkill settlement in Berks County by the 1750s. The two families were very much intermarried. The Northkill settlement was on both sides of the Northkill Creek, the majority living on the east side in Bern Township. The Melchior Detweiler and Hannes Miller families lived on the west side in Tulpehocken Township. In 1737, when Jacob Miller and Jacob Mast took out two warrants of 300 acres each,[2] the whole area was part of Lancaster County and the two townships were part of Tulpehocken.[3] Up to now it has been impossible to locate the Miller homestead in Berks County precisely. The location of the Hochstetler tracts is known, and that of Melchior Detweiler on the other side as well, but the Miller homestead continues to elude us.

There is a Hannes Miller who was a passenger on the ship *Phoenix* that came to Philadelphia on September 15, 1749, who a number of historians agree is probably our ancestor.[4] He has the name Hannes, which was used by him both in Berks and Somerset Counties. In addition to him, there were a number of other Amish-Mennonite immigrants on the same ship.

---

[1] Rev. Harvey Hostetler, *Descendants of Jacob Hochstetler, the Immigrant of 1736 (DJH)*, (Elgin, Ill.: 1912, reprint).

[2] Warrant Registry, Lancaster Co., Pa.

[3] See early Lancaster Co. map.

[4] Ralph B. Strassburger and William J. Hinke, *Pennsylvania German Pioneers* (Norristown, Pa.: Pennsylvania German Society, 1934).

Some of them became relatives by marriage, and others undoubtedly came from the same general area in Europe. The great majority were ethnic Swiss-German names from Canton Bern.

At least twenty-five names that can be identified as Amish-Mennonites were on the same ship and later appeared in the Northkill settlement. They can be compared with lists in Europe and included: Nafziger, Kurtz, Lantz, Fisher, Seiler, Mishler, and Berkey. Also on the ship was a man named Benedict Lehman whose name appears in the Berks community and near the Miller homestead in Somerset. Another Benedict Lehman was on a previous immigrant ship, the *Charming Nancy* in 1737. Interestingly, it was the first sizable group of Amish immigrants with names such as Mast, Beiler, Speicher, Hershberger, and Berkey. It also included Jacob and Barbara Miller and two single males, Abraham and Christian Miller.[5] Besides these there was a Benedict Lehman, a wife Ferona, and three children, including another Benedict.

Is there some connection between the Millers and Lehmans on the 1737 ship and the one that came in 1749? There was no John or Hannes Miller on the 1737 ship, but in spite of its being such a common name generally, there were only a few in the Northkill settlement and even fewer original warrants. One searches the plat maps in vain for the name of John Miller. A Nicholas Miller came on the ship *Brotherhood* in 1750. One must look for Millers among the other Amish-Mennonite names, lest some other Miller is chosen who has nothing to do with Amish. Nicholas Miller is readily seen as a member of the community. He has a warrant in Bern Township. When he died in 1784 his estate was signed by relatives and leaders of the Amish church. The same was true of Christian Miller who died in 1791 in Bern Township.[6] Nicholas later had a warrant in Somerset County just next to that of John Miller.[7] Nicholas came on a ship with other names such as Holly, Mast, Blough, Nafziger, and Berkey, illustrating the similarity of the names in the three ships that had Millers as passengers.[8] There were other names, but for the time being let us limit them to these examples.

Hannes, or John Miller, Sr., as he is officially called, was about nineteen years old when he came to America in 1749. If he had been the son of the Jacob Miller of 1737, he would have been only seven if he came with his parents. This is assuming that he was the son of the Jacob Miller of 1737, but was not listed on the ship list. Possibly the cut-off point on that one list might have been ten years or so, rather than sixteen. Then Benedict Lehman, Jr., who is listed, might have also come with the family of Benedict, Sr., but was old enough to be on the ship list. In this interpretation of events, John and Benedict, Jr., may have gone back to Europe in 1748 for various reasons: to look for a wife, perhaps to see relatives

---

[5] Abraham and Christian Miller could have been older children or relatives of Jacob since they are mentioned with him. The younger Benedict Lehman is named with his mother. This is one of the few ship lists that includes children's names. The usual cut-off for signing is sixteen years of age. This was on only one list of three where there was a different cut-off point.

[6] Will records, Reading, Berks Co., Pa.

[7] Plat map, Brothers Valley Twp., Somerset Co., Pa.

[8] Strassburger and Hinke.

who had been left behind, even to look after property or inheritance for their parents. At any rate, the names of Hannes Miller and Benedict Lehman, Jr., are increasingly linked together. The discovery of the presumed grave of Magdalena, wife of Hannes Miller, in Somerset County, raises the possibility that she may have been the daughter of Benedict Lehman, Sr., also too young to be on the 1737 ship list.

The Millers and Lehmans, among others, only stayed in Berks County about thirty-four years. In general the older generation did not migrate further west, unless it was a shorter distance to Lebanon County or to places nearer to Lancaster and Reading to be safe from the Indian raids. The raid in which the Hochstetlers were taken captive and some of them killed, and in which Hannes Miller was wounded by the Indians, took place during the French and Indian War in 1757. This was followed by a peace treaty in which the French and Indians surrendered their prisoners and all of western Pennsylvania to the Ohio border. Then the American Revolution against the English began about 1775. Before that, by 1770, a few Amish settlers began the movement across the Allegheny Mountains to Bedford, to the part which is now Somerset County. In the course of the French and Indian War, roads were built for the military, which made movement of goods much easier. The settlers were looking for new lands to settle where they would not be bothered by French, Indians, English, or Americans, who began to make demands on them to do military service in the American Revolution. This provided impetus for the Amish settlers, especially the younger ones, to look for new homes. When the British won the French and Indian War, the Indians were moved further west beyond the Ohio River.

John Miller wasn't the first to cross the Allegheny Mountains to Bedford (now Somerset) County, but he was a member of a delegation of Amish who went in 1771 and took out some of the earliest warrants in Bedford County. The only evidence we have for this are the names on a tax list, indicating that they had a warrant for land.[9] At that time Bedford County included not only Somerset County, but also some territories to the north which are now parts of other counties. The earliest warrants were kept in Bedford until 1795, when Somerset County was formed. Most of the early Amish warrants were in Brothers Valley Township, which was also much larger than now, comprising most of the southern half of present day Somerset County.

Hannes Miller's companions in 1771 were, among others, Nicholas and Michael Miller, who were probably his brother and nephew; Michael was the son of Jacob Miller. Others were neighbors from the Amish community in Berks County: John Hershberger, Christian Knege (Gnaegi), Pence (Benedict) Lehman, Peter Livengood, John Siler (Saylor), Christian Spiker (Speicher), Michael Troyer, Christian and Yost Zuck (Zug).[10] They all selected warrants in Brothers Valley Township, but some of them were located in present-day Elklick and Summit Townships, since they were then still part of Brothers Valley.

---

[9] Published *Pennsylvania Archives*, Tax Lists for Bedford Co., 1771.
[10] *Ibid.*

Deed showing the sale of land in Elklick Township, Bedford County, in 1775; document is in the Bedford County Courthouse. The land is now in Somerset County since 1795.

It is not completely clear where Hannes Miller's warrant was, but Benedict Lehman, Christian Speicher, and Nicholas Miller took up land in what is now known as the Glades, in the area just north of present day Berlin along the stream Stony Creek on both sides of the border between Brothers Valley and Stony Creek Townships. The tract that Hannes Miller occupied was first warranted to Christian Herr, which initially made the identification of John Miller's land difficult.[11] In fact, he may have settled in what is now Elklick Township to the south near the border of Maryland, where Peter Livengood, Yost Zug, and later the Masts, Hochstetlers, and Christners settled.

There is a warrant in the land records at Bedford that has Abraham Coxson selling a tract of 300 acres to John Miller of Berks County.[12] The location is near the land of John Hochstetler, who lived near him in Berks County. The date was 1775, four years later. John Miller's daughter Barbara was married to Jacob Hochstetler, oldest son of John Hochstetler. The Hochstetler history says that

---

[11] *Ibid.*
[12] Plat map of Brothers Valley Twp., Somerset Co., Pa. Early land warrants on records in Bedford Co. Courthouse.

Jacob and Barbara's oldest son John was born in 1776, so their marriage must have taken place about the time of that land purchase.

John Miller, Sr., had three older sons who could have helped him at first, although his oldest son, John, Jr., was also married at about the same time. John, Sr.'s next oldest sons, Jacob and Peter, were not yet married, so all of them must have at first helped with the clearing of this tract of 300 acres. The fact that Barbara, John, Jr., Jacob, and Peter all settled in southern Somerset County lends weight to the conclusion that John Miller, Sr.'s first home west of the Alleghenies was in Elklick Township. They all settled in the Casselman River area in what are now Elklick and Summit Townships.

Hannes Miller and his wife Magdalena had seven more children, all born in Berks County. The land warrants do not indicate by their dates the actual date of settling on the land. In fact, many of the warranted lands were not settled until years later. The warrantee did not obtain ownership of the land until it was surveyed and a patent was made for it. Some persons with warrants never lived in Somerset County. They either waited until one of their children took it over, or transferred it to someone else. John Miller paid taxes in 1771 and they may have been for the warrant in present day Brothers Valley Township. It is true that the tract first had the name of Christian Herr, but no one of that name appeared; the tract was called Miller's Choice, and it was in the Glades area of Brothers Valley Township.[13] It was near the Nicholas Miller, Christian Speicher, and Benedict Lehman farms. It is possible that John Miller knew Christian Herr back in Berks County, or even had some financial obligation to him which prevented him from taking his original warrant at first. Eventually a part of Hannes's family ended up in the Glades.

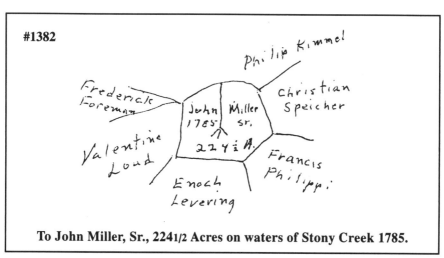

Drawing of plat #1382 issued to John Miller, Sr., in 1785 in Brothers Valley Township, Somerset County. Document in Somerset County Courthouse.

---

[13] Plat map of Brothers Valley Twp., Somerset Co., Pa.

When John Miller bought the Elklick tract from Coxson in 1775, he paid thirteen pounds for the land which, the document states, already had some improvements on it. In this case, the original warrant was to Abraham Coxson, who then chose to sell it. The improvements that were made may have meant clearing a bit of the land and erecting a cabin near a spring or source of water. In contrast, the tract bearing the name of Christian Herr may have been totally uncleared. It is not known at what date Coxson received his warrant.[14]

The transfer to John Miller was signed by Michael Buchele (Beegley) and Yost Yoder. Beegley's name comes on the tax list first in 1774.[15] He was the son-in-law of Christian Zug of Chester County, who became a kind of land agent for Amish and others. He was in the delegation in 1771 that selected land, but he never settled in Somerset County. Zug's son Yost did settle in Elklick Township. Beegley's name is also on the plat of Yost Yoder, just a bit northeast of the Miller-Coxson farm, and just opposite to the east of the Hochstetler farms. The deed in the possession of the present owner, who is a descendant of Yost Yoder, says "of Lancaster County." Yost never settled in Somerset County, but his son Henry did. Yet the plat map says Beeghel's Place, though he was only the land agent. Plat maps can be confusing.

The John Hochstetler family did not come to Somerset County until 1784, but John (who was the oldest son of the immigrant Jacob) and his oldest son Jacob paid taxes in what is now Elklick Township in 1779. Probably, although the whole family did not come until 1784, some of the men at least were engaged in clearing the land before that while the family remained in Berks County.[16]

Since the Hochstetler and Miller farms were near each other, John's son Jacob and his young wife, Barbara Miller, may have done some basic clearing or even built a log dwelling. The Millers also kept their property in Berks until the whole family migrated about 1775.

John Miller stayed in Elklick Township for only eleven years, if we assume that he came in 1775. In 1786 Peter Livengood was looking for a farm for his son Christian, the first of his twelve children to come of age. Peter Livengood was one of the first settlers to come to Elklick Township, coming with the same delegation in 1771 that the Millers came on. Livengood was a weaver and merchant who traveled to the various settlements in Berks and Lancaster Counties, selling cloth and articles necessary to frontier people, a kind of peddler. In the absence of other media, he no doubt brought news of the various communities. He first lived in Berks County near the Mennonites and Amish, where he began a journal which included his various sales and the names of the people he sold goods to. He, like Michael Beegley, joined the German Baptist Brethren (also called Dunkards or Church of the Brethren). They both became ministers, along with Christian Hochstetler, the brother of John, and youngest son of the immigrant Jacob. Christian also had a tract of land in Elklick Town-

---

[14] Coxson tract, on record at Bedford Co. Courthouse.
[15] Tax lists, Bedford Co., Pa., 1771.
[16] See tax lists, Bern Twp., Berks Co., Pa., 1779.

ship, south of the Millers, Livengoods, and the other Hochstetlers. Thus the community was mixed with both Dunkards and Amish, among others.

Peter Livengood's journal has been preserved and a notation at the time of his son Christian's marriage states that he bought the farm of John Miller, which appears to be the same farm John Miller bought from Abraham Coxson in 1775. The date was 1786. By that time Hannes's sons Hannes or John, Jr.,[17] Jacob, and Peter were married with children and farming for themselves. The next two sons, Christian and Joseph, were over twenty and capable of farming for themselves. There is a deed drawn up at about this time for the farm in the Glades originally with the name of Christian Herr. This time it bears the name of John Miller's son Christian, in whose name it was formally registered.[18] At the same time in the book of plats in the courthouse at Somerset there is a plat of the same farm, dated 1786, that bears the name of John Miller, Sr. It appears that he had the land resurveyed at the time, before making the deed out to his son Christian.[19] Besides the six children of John Miller, Sr., thus far named, there were five more, all girls. It appears that all these younger children, along with the parents, joined Christian and Joseph in the Glades. As will be seen by their marriages, all of these had spouses from the Glades or further north in the county.

These are the remaining six children who moved to the Glades:

5. **Christian Miller**, married Freny ___, up to now unidentified, but evidence points to her being the sister of Christian Blough, their neighbor in the Glades.[20] He was born ca1760.
6. **Joseph Miller**, born ca1762, was married first to Barbara Speicher, daughter of their neighbor, Christian Speicher, Sr.
7. **Catherine Miller**, who may have been older than Christian and Joseph, born ca1758, was married to Jacob Kauffman.
8. **Maria** or **Mary Miller**, born ca1764, was married to John Schrock, Jr., also their neighbor in the Glades.
9. **Veronica**, or **Freny Miller**, born ca1766, was married to Christian Speicher, Jr., son of next door neighbor Christian Speicher, Sr., and brother of Joseph's wife Barbara.
10. **(?Susanna) Miller**, born ca1768, married to Christian Mishler, son of Joseph Miller of the Glades. The name Susanna occurs in this family, thus the reason for suggesting it. Not documented.

Thus all the younger children moved to the Glades, where the property was maintained all along. It is not known to what extent the acreage was developed, or buildings built while they were living in Elklick Township. There is a tradition in the family of Jacob, the oldest or second-oldest son, that Jacob lived for some

---

[17] Peter Livengood's Journal, notation, 1786.
[18] Deed in possession of Thomas Maust, Berlin, Pa., the present owner.
[19] Plat map in the plat book, Somerset Co. Courthouse.
[20] Dr. Hugh F. Gingerich and Rachel W. Kreider, *Amish and Amish-Mennonite Genealogies (AAMG)* (Gordonville, Pa.: Pequea Publishers, 1986), #BL6, p. 27.

years in the Glades.[21] By the time Hannes and his younger children moved there in 1786, the four oldest children were all settled in Elklick or Summit Townships to the south.

Children of John Miller who stayed in Elklick and Summit Townships:[22]

1. **Barbara Miller**, born ca1750, was married to Jacob Hochstetler, oldest son of John Hochstetler, son of Immigrant Jacob. They lived south of Meyersdale in Summit Township.
2. **John Miller, Jr.**, born ca1752, was married to Freny Yoder, daughter of Christian Yoder of Bern Township, Berks County. They lived in Summit Township, south of the Casselman River, northwest of Meyersdale.
3. **Jacob Miller**, born ca1754, was married to Anna Stutzman, daughter of Christian Stutzman and Barbara Hochstetler, sister of John Hochstetler. They lived in Elklick Township, north of Springs, until they moved to Tuscarawas County, Ohio, in 1809.
4. **Peter Miller**, born ca1756, was married to Mary Stutzman, sister of Anna, wife of Jacob Miller. They lived in Summit Township, just south of Meyersdale, Pennsylvania.

---

[22] *AAMG*.
[21] Alta Elizabeth Schrock and Olen L. Miller, *Joel B. Miller History* (Scottdale, Pa.: 1960), p. 20.

Last Years of Hannes or John Miller, Sr.

*T*he last years of John Miller, Sr., were spent on his farm in Brothers Valley Township. They must have been tranquil years after the great moves of his life, first from Europe to America in 1749, then the stay in Berks County. This stay must have been about twenty-five years, if we think of him as born ca1730, coming to America at age nineteen, getting married, and having most of his children until the move to Somerset County in 1775 or so.

Then there was the period in Elklick Township as the children were growing. The move to the Glades was preceded by the movement of his older sons to help clear the land, while the parents and part of the family were developing the land in Elklick Township. John thought of the Glades farm as a place for Christian and Joseph, and perhaps intended the Coxson tract for the older sons. But as these sons grew older, they wished to go on their own. Barbara and her husband, Jacob Hochstetler, John, Jr., Jacob, and Peter all got farms after 1790. Christian and Joseph had gone to the Glades farm. At this point he had the offer of Peter Livengood to buy his farm, and Hannes took him up on it and sold it.

Thus began the last period in which John and the four remaining daughters moved to Brothers Valley. He found that he soon had no children at home as the girls gradually got married. They lived nearby for the most part, and the two sons did the farming. In 1786 Hannes put the farm in Christian's name, for which he had to resurvey it and get a proper patent in order to transfer it to his son. John and his wife stayed on the Glades farm until they died.

In 1798 Hannes made his will and shortly after died. His will is one of the oldest filed in Somerset, since the county was only formed in 1795. His son Hannes, Jr., was the executor and Joseph Speicher, his son-in-law, assisted. In the estate papers which are filed, his wife Magdalena renounces the right to execute the will. Then follow the signatures of the officials of the court and the executor and witnesses. Magdalena must have stayed there until her death in 1817. By that time Joseph and Christian were ready to move north to what was first Quemahoning Township, and later Jenner and Conemaugh. There seemed to be a general movement in that direction because two of their sisters and their husbands also settled in Conemaugh Township. Hannes, Sr., and his wife lived together in the Glades only from 1786 to 1798, twelve years, although Magdalena lived another nineteen years. Hannes died at about age sixty-eight, an average age for that time, but not a great age.

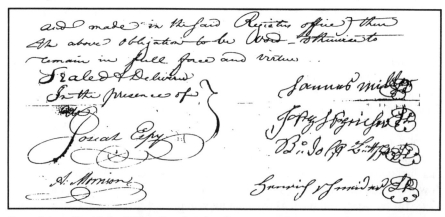

Document showing renunciation of serving as executor of her husband's estate, by Magdalena Miller, his widow. Somerset County Courthouse, 1798.

Part of the will of John Miller, Sr., showing signatures of executors Hannes Miller (Junior), Joseph Speicher, and officials of the courthouse in 1798.

Location of the
Miller Homesteads

*T*he other Millers associated with John Miller, Sr., were a father and a mother, Jacob and Barbara Miller, who came to Philadelphia on the ship *Charming Nancy* on October 8, 1737. Others have called this ship the *Amish Mayflower*, because although it may not have brought the very first Amish, it was the ship with a sizable number of people who could be first identified as Amish.

The Millers were sandwiched in the middle of the list with other known Amish, so Jacob and Barbara can reasonably be said to have been Amish. A historian has unearthed the account of the voyage by one of the passengers, John Jacob Kauffman, telling of the difficulties of the voyage which could take from six weeks to three months, depending on the delays in England for customs and the need to depend on the wind to sail the ship. Illness and even death could be expected for the immigrants to America in those days. Children especially died of illnesses that could not be treated adequately. [23]

This ship was unusual in that women and children were included on the list. The only other Millers were Abraham and Christian, named just after Jacob, presumably single. Though a list of women and children was included, there is no way of knowing whether there was some younger cut-off point rather than the usual age of sixteen. Children below that age were not named. If the Hannes Miller who came to America in 1749 at age nineteen came with his parents in 1737, he would have been only seven. As mentioned previously, Benedict Lehman, the fellow settler of Hannes Miller in both Berks and Somerset Counties, is named on both of these ships. [24]

It is likely that the second Benedict was Benedict, Jr., as the first Benedict died in Berks County and there were at least three Benedicts in three generations. Did Hannes Miller and his friend Benedict go back to Europe, perhaps in 1748, and return in 1749? It's a big "maybe." Otherwise, why would seven-year-olds stay in Europe for twelve years while the parents migrated to America? Or should we try some other hypothesis? Gingerich, in *AAMG*, in his footnote on the origins

---

[23] S. Duane Kauffman, *Mifflin County Amish and Mennonite Story* (Mifflin Co. Mennonite Hist. Soc., 1991), chapter 2.
[24] Strassburger and Hinke.

of the Amish-Mennonite Millers, also uses some of these same arguments but does not try to name the immigrant father. Instead, he puts most of the Northkill Millers into one family as brothers which, while physically possible, extends considerably the number of conjectures without documentation. [25]

The idea of returning to Europe was not uncommon, especially for those who acted as promoters of immigration. It was, however, an arduous trip even for younger, single men. In some cases the reason was to take care of some elderly relative, to enable them to join the family in America. Another motive might be to go back to get a wife. These are all conjectures.

One of the earliest clues to Jacob Miller as the progenitor of at least part of the Amish-Mennonite Millers was an application for land dated 1737 and registered in Lancaster. [26] At that time Berks County was part of Lancaster (until 1750), so the earliest applications and warrants for the area of Berks County are in Lancaster. This 1737 application was for Jacob Miller and it was on the Northkill Creek. One could easily dismiss it and say it must be some other Jacob Miller.

But wait, there was another application the same week for Jacob Mast and it was also in Tulpehocken Township on the Northkill Creek. This couldn't be a coincidence. But Jacob Mast's 1754 warrant was in Bern Township, east of the Northkill Creek, where he actually settled, which makes it likely that this Jacob Miller was also Amish. It was a puzzle until I found out that Tulpehocken Township included Bern Township at that time. Up to that time it had always been said that Bern Township was the original settlement, and that it later expanded to Tulpehocken, at least among the Amish. However, if warrants were

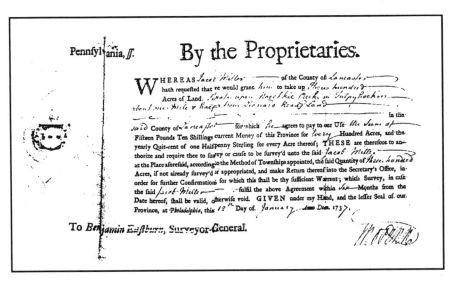

Application for land issued in 1737 to Jacob Miller. Lancaster County Courthouse.

---

[25] *AAMG.*
[26] Land applications, Lancaster Co., Pa.

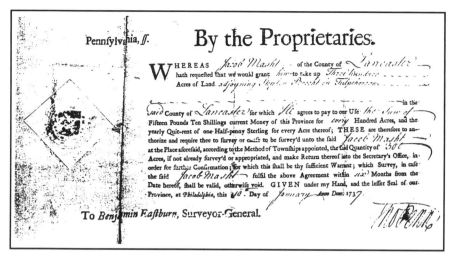

Application for land issued in 1737 to Jacob Mast. Lancaster County Courthouse.

issued before 1750, they would all have been Tulpehocken Township, Lancaster County. The date for the applications of Jacob Miller and Jacob Mast is also askew, because Jacob Miller's application was dated January 12 and Jacob Mast's was January 10, but the ship did not arrive in Philadelphia until October 8!

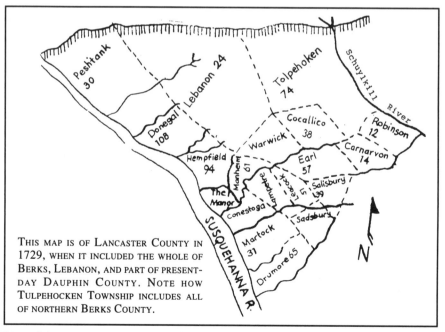

Map of the original Tulpehocken Township, Lancaster County, showing inclusion of all of Northkill settlement in Tulpehocken Township, and all of Berks County in Lancaster County (until 1750).

I discovered that in 1737 Tulpehocken Township was not only part of Lancaster County, but covered the whole area of the Northkill settlement, on both sides of the Northkill Creek. So the warrant could have included Jacob Mast's later place of settlement on the east side of the Northkill. I noticed that the very same tract that Jacob Mast took up in 1754, if added to the plats of Jacob Kauffman and Hans Lantz which were adjacent tracts next to Jacob Mast's 1754 warrant which mentions the 1737 warrant, makes a total of 291 acres, almost the exact amount of the 300 acres of the application. [27]

Taking that clue and applying it to the Millers just north of Masts, we find the warrant of Christian Miller, whom *AAMG* calls MLD and sees no relation to the other Millers. Like the Masts, there are other names associated with the plat issued to Christian Miller. Some of it was issued to Henry Stehley first and reverted to Christian Miller, while adjacent tracts were issued first to Henry Stehley who retained it, and another to Christian Stehley. Again, if one adds all the tracts issued to Millers and Stehleys, the total is 309 acres, or almost the same acreage as Jacob Miller's original application.

Ulrich Stehley, presumably the father of Henry and Christian, was a fellow passenger of Jacob Miller on the *Charming Nancy* in 1737. The two clusters of tracts are east of the Northkill Creek, but near enough for the issuing agent to claim that they were located "on the Northkill." This is a possible solution to the mystery of the 1737 applications. Christian Miller was the only Miller living there when the early tax lists appeared, but there are other associations. [28] Nicholas, the supposed brother of John Miller, Jr., is said to have been married to the daughter, or perhaps sister, of Henry Stehley. Among the executors of his Berks County will in 1784 were his wife Barbara and Henry Stehley, probably his brother-in-law. Somehow the 300-acre Miller tract came to be divided between Millers and Stehleys, and Nicholas found a farm a bit to the east, of ninety-five acres in Centre Township, where he presumably lived at the time he died in 1784. [29]

Nicholas also had a tract of land in Tulpehocken Township issued in 1752, left to Christian Miller in 1815. [30] Perhaps this was the farm that John Miller was working on when he was wounded by the Indians. No warrant to him in Tulpehocken Township has yet been discovered, although Hannes Miller is listed as a taxpayer in Tulpehocken in 1767. [31]

What is the meaning of all this? It means that the 300-acre tract was in Bern Township when the application was issued. But how could the application be made if the person making it had not yet arrived? It is possible that someone arriving the year before, such as their future neighbor Melchior Detweiler, was authorized by Miller and Mast to make such an application for them. At any rate, the two applications were located in the middle of the later Northkill settlement,

---

[27] *Early Amish Land Grants in Berks County, Pennsylvania* (Gordonville, Pa.: Pequea Bruderschaft Library, 1990).
[28] *AAMG*, section on Millers.
[29] Will of Nicholas Miller, Courthouse, Reading, Berks Co., Pa.
[30] Land records, Berks Co., Pa.
[31] Tax records, Berks Co., in *Pennsylvania Archives* (published).

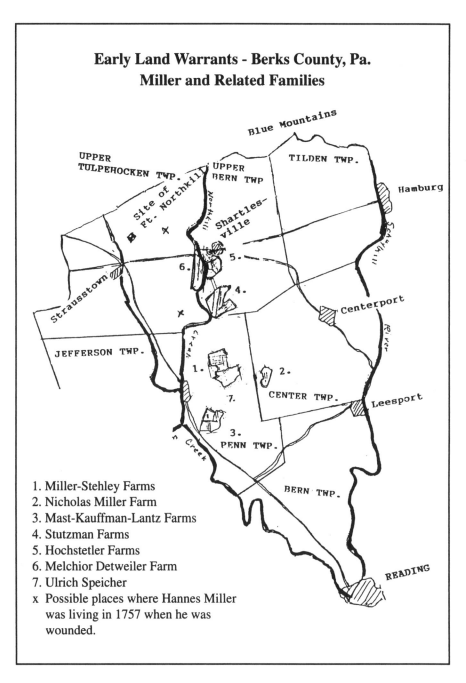

Map of the northern part of Berks County (present borders) showing the Amish-Mennonite farms relating to the location of the Miller homesteads.

if the above reasoning has any reliability. That would make the children of Jacob Miller, the immigrant of 1737: Christian Miller, identified as MLD by *AAMG*; Nicholas Miller because of his relation to the Stehleys; John Miller our ancestor; and the Jacob Miller who accompanied him and Nicholas to Somerset County in 1771 as the four siblings. It is possible that the latter two had no warrants in Berks County, but simply worked on the family estates. This makes an entirely new division of the Miller family from that proposed by *AAMG*.[32]

John could presumably have been working in Tulpehocken Township as noted above at the time of the Hochstetler massacre in 1757. Christian could have been the older son of Jacob Miller named on the *Charming Nancy* in 1737, and John and Nicholas were younger children not named on the ship list. A further possibility would be that they were nephews or stepchildren who came later, in 1749 and 1750. There definitely is some connection.

One unaccounted for Miller not named in *AAMG* is Christian Miller. I think we can't ignore him because he came on the same ship with the three Yoders who are the ancestors of most of the Amish Yoders in America. The same can be said for the three Zug-Zook immigrants, Christian, Johannes, and Moritz; also, Johannes Gnaegi, Johannes Gerber, and Jacob Kurtz, all named together, and Christian Miller is in the midst of them. This looks like the Christian named by *AAMG* as ML5, the younger brother of John Miller, Sr., numbered as ML2. But if that is true, the Christian who came in 1742 would have been only two years old, to be their sibling. Christian is said to have been married first to a Gnaegi and then to a Mishler. He would not have been on the ship list if he was less than sixteen.[33]

There is a generation missing somewhere, and this underlines the fact that *AAMG* has too many Millers in one family. It wavers on the name of the father of the first generation of Millers and puts a ? before the name Christian. I say there are two groups: a Jacob group and a Christian group. The Christian Miller who came in 1742 was obviously more than two years old, so it appears to me that there was a Christian Miller, Sr., married to a Gnaegi, probably the sister of fellow passenger Johannes Gnaegi, and a Christian, Jr., who later married Freny Mishler. Freny came to America with her family in 1749 and was therefore similar in age to Christian, Jr.

Would Christian, Sr., have any other children? Yes, in my opinion, Samuel, Peter, and probably Abraham of the supposed brothers of John Miller, Sr. In addition, there is a Jacob who had land adjacent to Christian Miller in Cumru Township, Berks County. I like to call him Christian of Cumru in contrast to Jacob of Bern Township. With this arrangement, all the Cumru group settled for a time in Cumru Township, while the Jacob group settled in Bern and Tulpehocken Townships. It is true that Samuel (ML6) and Peter (ML3) lived in Bern Township for a while, but they later moved to Cumru Township.

---

[32] Compare with *AAMG*, p. 269.
[33] Strassburger and Hinke.

The research of Paul Lefever has shown that descendants of Abraham Miller (ML7) lived in Berks and Lancaster Counties other than Bern Township, and has added a revision of the children of Abraham and a new son, John.[34] Although many of the Cumru group's descendants also moved to Somerset County, almost all of them tended to go to the northern townships of Conemaugh and nearby townships directly, rather than Elklick and Brothers Valley. This regrouping allows for duplication of names, such as two Christians and two Jacobs. Christian (ML5), who has a son Abraham, is in the same grouping as ML7 (Abraham, father, and son). I think the two groups are related, but it would have to go back to European lines, e.g., Jacob and Christian might be brothers.

There are several Anabaptist Miller families not yet accounted for, but these two are the main ones. This history is of only the Jacob group through John, Sr. I have not examined the land records for Christian of Cumru except for the plat maps published by the Lancaster County Amish, John Mark Slabaugh, and Masthof Press.[35] I think this discussion does not contradict most of their findings. They do not mention the 300-acre applications of Jacob Miller and Jacob Mast in 1737.

Earlier I had made a sketch map of the same area and it is generally in agreement with it, though it does not have the precision of the Slabaugh drawings. I have a few that they do not have, and I question a few of the ones on their maps as perhaps not Amish. There is an unidentified Jacob Miller with a tract adjacent to that of Christian of Cumru. Is he perhaps another son of Christian, Sr., who came in 1742? The Jacob who came with John Miller, Sr., to Somerset County in 1771 I place with the Jacob group because of his will made in Somerset County in 1801 which links him to John, Jr., and his sons Yost and David.

---

[34] Paul Lefever, "John Miller, an Amish Minister?" *Mennonite Family History (MFH)* Oct. 1990.

[35] *Early Amish Land Grants.*

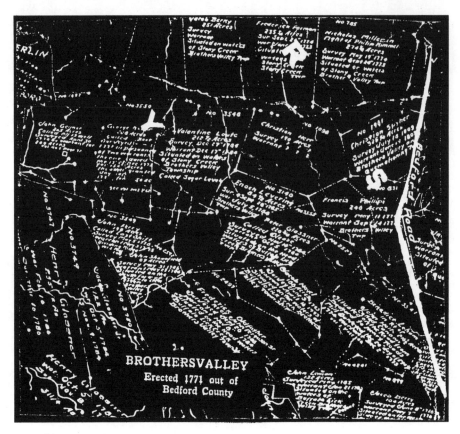

Part of the official plat map (a later compilation of individual plats registered in the Somerset and Bedford County Courthouses). Note that the warrants are very uneven in date, and some, like that of Christian Herr, have no date or information like acreage, and are the same as the plat of 1785 issued to John Miller, Sr.

Locating the John Miller, Sr.,
Homestead in Brothers Valley in the Glades

For a long time the Miller homestead in Somerset County was not known. It was not even known that John Miller, Sr., came to Somerset County, though the early tax records have his name. The account in the Hochstetler book by Moses B. Miller does not tell where he lived, yet there is a record of the settlement of John's estate in the Somerset County Courthouse, dated 1798.[36] I found this to put into my history of the descendants of my great-grandfather, Daniel B. Miller, in 1970. Even with that information, I was unable to find the Brothers Valley farm. I found the farm of his son, John, Jr., on the south side of the Casselman River in Summit Township. On the other side of the river was the farm of Yost, the son of John, Jr., and my ancestor, who came to Ohio in 1816.[37] Yost sold it to Abraham Miller before moving to Ohio. These were found by using the plat map of the township and comparing the names with subsequent owners, if it only had the name of the original warrantee.[38]

By the same method I found the original homesteads of John, Sr.'s sons Jacob in Elklick Township and Peter in Summit Township. On the top of a hill at the south edge of Meyersdale was the homestead of Barbara, John, Sr.'s oldest child, married to Jacob Hochstetler, son of John. Just who gave the information that John, Jr., moved to Ohio in 1815 is uncertain, but *DJH* says that the account of Moses B. Miller was supplemented by Hochstetler historian William F. Hochstetler, and he is perhaps responsible for giving that information.

What is now obvious is that John Miller, Jr.'s estate settlement is also on file in Somerset, only three years after his father's, in 1802. He died as a relatively young man, at age fifty, and his two sons, Yost and David, were his executors. It was John, Jr.'s brother Jacob, who was one of the first settlers in Tuscarawas County, Ohio, in 1809 after a stay of only twenty-nine years in Somerset County. Another early will was that of Jacob Miller who, from the information about his estate, was a younger brother of John Miller, Sr.[39]

---

[36] Will in Somerset Co. Courthouse.
[37] Virgil Miller, *Miller Family History* (1970).
[38] Plat maps of Elklick, Summit, and Brothers Valley Twps., Somerset Co., Pa.
[39] Wills on record, Somerset Co. Courthouse.

Attic of the Thomas Maust home near Berlin, Pennsylvania, showing the log beams and chimney on the John Miller, Sr., homestead. It could be part of the original house, but that fact can't be proven at the present time.

Jacob first asked John, Jr., to be his executor in 1801 when it was made, but then there is the notation that John, Jr., died in 1802. With that, the two young sons of John, Jr., Yost, age twenty-five, and David, age twenty-two, became the executors. It is not stated why Michael, son of Jacob Miller, was not made executor as he must have been older than the sons of his cousin, John, Jr.[40]

Thus we have known for a number of years that John Miller, Sr., died in Somerset County. The estate settlement does not say where he lived. John, Sr.,'s name does not appear on the Somerset County plat maps.[41] It was Paul V. Hostetler, a persistent historian of the Hochstetler-Hostetler family, who located the farm in Brothers Valley Township in the middle of the Glades settlement on the stream known as Stony Creek. He found that the farm on the plat map under the name of Christian Herr was really for John Miller, Sr. On the map his next-door neighbors were Nicholas Miller and Christian Speicher, just as we would

---

[40] Registry of Wills, Somerset Co. Courthouse, Somerset, Pa.
[41] Plat map of original plats, Brothers Valley Twp.

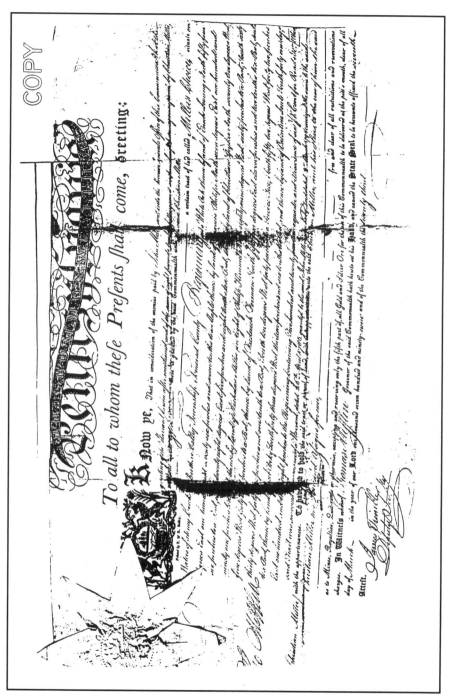

Reduced copy of the deed transferring the ownership of the Brothers Valley farm to John Miller, Sr.'s son Christian in 1785. The original deed is in the possession of the farm's present owner, Thomas Maust, Sr.

expect from the tax records, and his friend Benedict Lehman was only a few farms away.

I was teaching in Saudi Arabia at the time and one summer Paul took me to the farm. We met Thomas Maust, the owner, and his son Tom, Jr., who was a college student at the time and was genuinely interested in the history of the farm. We went to see the farm cemetery, which has a single legible gravestone. It says "M1817M," which appears to be that of Magdalena, wife of John, Sr. The gravestone of John, Sr. is no longer there. Mr. Maust showed us the house where, when we were taken to the attic, we saw that it was an original log house with very thick wooden walls covered with white clapboard. He then showed us a deed of 1786 in which it showed John Miller, Sr., transferring the farm to his son Christian.[42]

Since that time, about 1975, many people have visited the homestead and Tom Maust, Jr. Wrote a fine article about the Glades Amish settlement for the Berlin Centennial in 1976.[43] Berlin is the principal town of Brothers Valley Township. The Maust farm is without doubt the homestead of John Miller, Sr., Hannes Miller, Indian John, Crippled John, or Wounded John. Whatever you want to call him, he is the same person. In 1997 I spent some time at the Somerset County Courthouse. After all those years of obscurity, imagine my surprise when, as I was paging through the older volumes of the plat book, I found Plat #1382, issued to John Miller, Sr., in 1786, with the same neighbors as the Christian Herr plat, on the waters of Stony Creek. The plat map was wrong![44] Who was Christian Herr?

---

[42] Deed in the possession of Thomas Maust, Berlin, Pa.
[43] Thomas Irvin Maust II, "The Glades Amish of Brothersvalley," *Bicentennial Book of Berlin, Pa.* (1976).
[44] Plat map of original plats, Brothers Valley Twp.

Ancestry of John Miller, Sr., As Reconstructed From the Sources

John Miller, Sr., sometimes called Hannes, was born in Europe, most likely in a village in the Palatinate in Germany. The family originated in Canton Bern, Switzerland. They belonged to the strict group of Anabaptists under the leadership of Jakob Amman, known in America as Amish-Mennonites. As dissenters from the state church, they had to leave Switzerland. In 1697 Henry Muller's name appears on a list of Anabaptists in Ste. Marie-aux-Mines, Alsace, the place where Jacob Amman led a group of refugees from Switzerland. The 1697 list was one of the earliest.[45]

A few years later, in 1699, the name of Johannes Müller is found in a citation from the authorities in Zweibrücken, Germany, with Hans Witwer, that they were tenants at the farm villages of Dusenbrücken and Huberhof near Pirmasens.[46] The text said that they came from Markirch (German for Ste. Marie) and that after a short time they were expelled back to Alsace. In 1703 the name of Johannes Müller appears on a list of Anabaptist followers of Jacob Amman in St. Marie-aux-Mines.[47] In two other lists of 1704 and 1708 the name does not appear, indicating both Johannes and Henry had left. Though Müller is a very common name in German-speaking areas, among the Amish it was not very common at the time.

Another citation, this time from the Jura region of Switzerland, has Heini, or Hainest Müller again listed in a group of Anabaptists in what was then the Bishopric of Basel, at that time not under the rule of Canton Bern.[48] It is ironic that the Catholic bishop, who was the ruler of that territory, was more tolerant of the Anabaptists than the Protestant rulers of Canton Bern. It was a short distance from Bern in the part of present day Canton Bern where French is spoken. At that time it was a safe haven not so far from their original homes.

---

[45] Archives du Haut-Rhin, Colmar, Alsace, List of Anabaptists, 1697.
[46] Ernst Drumm, *Zur Geschichte der Mennoniten im Herzogtum Pfalz-Zweibrücken* (Zweibrücken, 1962), p. 29.
[47] *Ibid.*, List of 1703, Ste. Marie-aux-Mines, Alsace.
[48] Archives of the Bishopric of Basel, Switzerland, Porrentruy, Sw. List of Anabaptists in the Bishopric of Basel, 1727.

Heini or Henry Müller was from Mützig or Münsingen, a town on the Aar River between Bern and Thun. He was living at La Heutte in the Bishopric of Basel in 1730, age sixty, with his nephew Christian Knegi, age thirty-two, married to Frene Cophet (Kauffman), thus born ca1698; Henry would have been born ca1670. His name was really Heinrich, with the shortened form Heini, and the French form of it is Henri or Henry, as it was written in Ste. Marie. Now we can follow their route: born at Münsingen, then Ste. Marie in 1697, and back in the Bishopric of Basel in 1730, age sixty. The village was given where he was born near Münsingen, called Tägertschi. Just to test the validity of this record, I decided to look at the local records at Münsingen. I found the following:

Births:	1667 - Hans, son of Christen Müller and Elsbeth Frey.
	1669 - Heinrich, son of Christen Müller and Elsbeth Frey.
	1674 - Barbara, daughter of Christen Müller and Elsbeth Frey.
	1698 - Christen, son of Hans Gnägi and Barbara Müller.
Marriage:	1666 - Christen Müller and Elsbeth Frey. [49]

These statistics tell a lot. Heinrich (Henri in French) is the same person who was in Ste. Marie-aux-Mines, Alsace, in 1697 (age twenty-eight). He is the same person who returned to the Bishopric of Basel (sometimes called the Jura region because of the Jura Mountains), age sixty. With him was his nephew Christian Knegi, age thirty-two. Again, the Münsingen record fits exactly. Heinrich Müller had a brother Hans and a sister Barbara, who later married Hans Gnägi and had a son Christen, born 1698. Again, it fits. Even the family name Gnägi or Knegi fits, for Miller and Gnaegi families have lived near each other and intermarried in America.

That leaves the brother, Hans or Johannes. Since both Hans and Heinrich Müller were in Ste. Marie-aux-Mines, and the Swiss record has them as brothers, it appears to me that this may be the Hans Müller who came north to the Palatinate, since he already made one attempt in 1699. But where did this Hans Müller go next? Did he go back to the Jura region near his home with his brother Heini? There is an intriguing item in the records of the *Taüferkammer*, a bureau of the government in Bern to take care of Anabaptist affairs. It was set up when the government made a rule that everyone had to be baptized into the state church, the Swiss Reformed. The method of baptism was as infants, which the Anabaptists rejected, and they insisted on having their own church services. There is a record of the *Täuferkammer*, dated 1727 from Tägertschi again, that Hans and Daniel Müller had been cited by the *Täuferkammer* about a property belonging to Nicolaus Egli; and Mädli Müller of Tägertschi was cited just for being a *Wiedertäufer*, that is, an Anabaptist. Did Hans Müller attempt to come back to Münsingen to see about the property?[50] There are other examples of persons coming back, and then going again into exile.

---

[49] Gemeinde-Register, Münsingen, Switzerland.
[50] Records of the *Täuferkammer*, State Archives, Bern, Switzerland.

Whether the above is relevant to the ancestry of our Miller family cannot be proven at this time, but elements of the facts, the dates, and the names make me think there is some connection. The next place that Anabaptist Müllers appear is in the Palatinate again. They were uneasy in Alsace because the King, Louis XIV, was trying to make laws forbidding people in France from practicing any religion except Catholic. The wars against the Huguenots in France were essentially between Catholics and Protestants and the Catholic party had won. Alsace was newly annexed to France, and many local princes wanted to keep their Anabaptist farmers. But they definitely did not welcome them to increase their numbers, so many Anabaptists prepared to move again to more tolerant places. At that time the German states were more tolerant.

In the early 1700s many Anabaptists were moving into Baden across the Rhine, the parts of Alsace not yet under the French, and the Palatinate to the north. About 1740, just before our ancestors began to emigrate to America, there were groups of both Mennonites and Amish in the Palatinate. They had ministers and worship services, but they were widely scattered. Two of the Anabaptists likely to be related to us were in the district of Lautern in 1717. They were Jakob and Nikel Müller, and the area where they lived as refugees was the area between Kaiserslautern and the French border at Wissembourg. There were some little principalities on the French border which allowed Anabaptists to live there. A church was gradually formed, with people on farms on both sides of the border.[51]

At the Palatine Archives in Speyer are records of leaseholders of farms in the southern Palatinate. At Mülhofen near Landau, there is a certificate of rental (*Bestandsbriefe*) issued to Adam Kurtz in 1713, the year the French king issued the decree that all non-Catholics were to be expelled from France. He was followed in 1714 by Jacob Kurtz and Claus Müller, and in 1723 it was issued to Adam Kurtz and Nicolaus Müller. In 1732 it was Jacob Kurtz and Consort, and in 1756 it was Jacob Holly and Johann Müller. In 1787 it was Daniel Holly and Peter Danner.

In 1750 Jacob Holly wanted to take over the farm of his brother-in-law Jacob Müller, as Müller had found another place. This item forms the basis for my belief that our Miller immigrants of 1737, 1742, 1749, and 1750 came from Mühlhofen and vicinity.[52] This also fits with some of the Müllers found in the Palatine Mennonite Census Lists. Mülhofen was in the part of the Palatine that was ruled by Zweibrücken at that time, and wasn't included in the census. But Ernst Drumm has compiled a small book with notations about Anabaptists in that area which contains a few items about Müllers.

In 1764, for example, Jacob Müller from the district of Eusserthal, was married to Elisabetha, the daughter of the deceased leaseholder of Hilschbacherhof, Michael Müller. Here is an example of two branches of Anabaptist Müllers inter-marrying.[53] Nikel, Claus, or Nicolaus Müller reminds us that Nicholas Miller appears to be the brother of our ancestor, John Miller, Sr.

---

[51] State Archives, Speyer, Palatinate, Germany.
[52] *Bestandsbriefe* (Rental Agreements), State Archives, Speyer, Germany.
[53] Drumm, op. cit., p. 45.

Information can also be gleaned from the *Palatine Mennonite Census Lists*. In 1745 Jacob Müller moved to Mörzheim, not far from Mühlhofen. He was probably of the Mühlhofen Müller family. Later Jakob Müller moved to Altamauer, northwest of Kaiserslautern, and his son Jacob came to Münsterhof, a well-known Amish-Mennonite hof. In 1744 at Hilsbach near Eusserthal, Jacob Müller took over the lease for his brother, Christian Müller, who had left for "the new land." [54] The new land could mean America, and this sounds like the Christian Miller who came to Pennsylvania in 1742. Johann Müller of Mühlhofen was mentioned above as having died in 1756, leaving his wife, the former Barbara Rogy, and minor children Johannes, Magdalena, and Catharina. Catharina's guardian was named as Jakob Müller; Johannes's guardian was Velten (Valentine) Güngerich; and Magdalena's was Jacob Müller, the leaseholder. The document does not say where the deceased Johann Müller had been living, though it probably was at Mülhofen. [55]

Can we find anything useful for emigration history from this list of Müller names and places? I think we can because we are dealing with a very small number of families in a very limited area and describing a group that believed very strongly in marriage within the group. Many names were duplicated, since by the second or third generation and the limited number of Christian names used, it was inevitable. All these families were in the Amish-Mennonite congregation whose minister was Christian Holly, who came from Kurzenberg near Oberdiessbach in Switzerland, not far from Münsingen, the home of the Müllers. He came to Germany in 1718 and lived at Bärbelsteinerhof near Erlenbach, not far from the French border. [56] It was on the farm hof of a castle which had a long line of Anabaptist tenants. He must have been the pastor of the families at Mühlhofen. Some records of marriage and death were found a number of years ago in the Catholic parish book of Niederschlettenbach nearby. Two important marriages for this history are:

1729 -   Marriage of Johannes Nafziger and Barbara Holli.
         Marriage of Jakob Holli and Anna Müller. [57]

Jakob Holli was the person mentioned above as the brother-in-law of Jakob Müller. Johannes Nafziger married the daughter of Christian Holli and later became his successor as elder of the Amish-Mennonites in that area. He is the one who called two general ministers' meetings in 1759 and 1779, by which we can learn the locations of all the existing Amish-Mennonite churches at that time and the names of their ministers, a very good guide for the family history of that group. [58]

---

[54] Hermann and Gertrud Guth and J. Lemar and Lois Ann Mast, *Palatine Mennonite Census Lists, 1664-1793* (Elverson, Pa.: Mennonite Family History, 1987).
[55] Speyer Archives, Ausfautheiakten Mühlhofen, Nr. 60.
[56] J. Virgil Miller, "Hof Bärbelstein," *Mennonite Family History*, Jan. 1985.
[57] Catholic Parish book, Niederschlettenbach, Palatinate.
[58] Paul Showalter, "Die Essinger Konferenzen von 1759 und 1779," *Mennonitische Geschichtsblätter*, Dec. 1938, p. 49.

Thus Müllers were living at basically two locations in the Palatinate in the first half of the eighteenth century: at Mühlhofen and nearby villages, and at Hilschbacherhof near Eusserthal, a former cloister, both the possessions of the Bishopric of Speyer (Catholic). Another place was Mechtersheimerhof near Speyer, as well as a number of individual farm hofs, including the castle at Bärbelstein. Related families were Holly, Kurtz, Nafziger, Burcky, Joder, and Güngerich. All of these were found in eighteenth-century Pennsylvania.

The most likely location for the Millers who came to Pennsylvania in 1737 is Mühlhofen. The Johannes Müller who died in 1756 was likely the uncle of John Miller, Sr. Jacob Miller, who came in 1737, would then be the brother of the John who died in 1756 and they would be the sons of Nicholas Miller, Sr. The Jacob who negotiated with Jacob Holly about the lease to the Mühlhofen farm, moved to nearby Mörzheim, where he was living in 1753.[59] He had a son Jacob, born 1749, and some time after 1753 they moved north to Altamauer, near Kirchheimbolanden. Jacob, the son, then joined Jacob Hochstättler and David Holly on the Münsterhof near Dreisen. Jacob Hochstättler was the son of Isaak, the nephew of the immigrant Jacob Hochstetler, and served as an Amish-Mennonite bishop at Münsterhof.[60]

Why did Jacob Müller of Mühlhofen not bring his whole family to America in 1737 if he was the father of John Miller, Sr.? The answer is uncertain, but there are a few possible explanations. One is that John may have come to America as a child of seven, and went back to Europe when he was eighteen, returning the next year with another group of Amish immigrants, including his friend Benedict Lehman, who also came in 1737 and 1749. Or, Jacob the father may have been married twice, and John and Nicholas, the oldest sons, stayed in Mühlhofen with their grandfather, the elder Nicholas, Or, Nicholas died and John and Nicholas went to settle the estate or to get their inheritance. Another frequent reason for returning is to find a wife, but if John, Sr., married the daughter of Benedict Lehman, he had no reason to do this. Another possibility is that the parents of John, Sr., decided to return to Europe, which might explain why they have no further record of living in Pennsylvania.

---

[59] *Palatine Mennonite Census Lists.*
[60] See *MFH*, Apr. 1989.

The original farm of Barbara Miller and Jacob Hochstetler surrounded by the urban area of Meyersdale, Pennsylvania. Photo by J. Virgil Miller.

I. The Family of Barbara Miller and Jacob Hochstetler
Oldest Child of John Miller, Sr.

Barbara Miller, the oldest child of John Miller, was born about 1750 in Berks County, Pennsylvania. It is probable that her parents were living in Upper Tulpehocken Township on uncleared land that they were getting ready for farming. At the time her father was wounded by the Indians in 1757, the territory west of the Northkill Creek was no doubt a real wilderness. There is no indication that they moved at that time, though they may have left temporarily during the fighting between the British and the French with their Indian allies.

Fort Northkill was a short distance away. After the French and Indian War, Barbara was married to Jacob Hochstetler, the oldest son of John Hochstetler, their neighbor across the Northkill Creek, about 1775. In those early years it is difficult to tell whether they were living in Berks or Somerset County, as the Hochstetlers held land in both until after 1780. As the first farm that John Miller actually lived on appears not to have been in Elklick Township, Somerset, it is likely that they lived in both places. The men were perhaps engaged in clearing land, and at least some of the women stayed back in Berks County, especially those with small children. This was the case with Barbara and her husband Jacob who, when they did move to Somerset County, likely first helped to clear the land of both the Hochstetlers and the Millers.

It was in 1785 that Barbara and her husband took out a warrant for land near Meyersdale for 168 1/4 acres on a hill just south of Myersdale.[61] This move cut them off from the other Hochstetlers and Millers, who were then mostly living in Elklick Township to the south. Then Barbara's brother, Peter Miller, bought the land of Hugh Robinson just next to their land to the southwest, along the Casselman River. Barbara and Jacob soon had other neighbors with names such as Meyers, Fike, Klingaman, and Arnold, as well as Millers, Saylors, and Gnageys. It is probable that the parents never left the Amish Church, but as their children married in the community, they were attracted in other directions.

---

[61] *Pennsylvania Archives*, tax records. Also, land records, Somerset Co., Pa. See also *Descendants of Jacob Hochstetler*, #3 ff. *(DJH)*.

Barbara and Jacob's tract was called Deer Pasture on the warrant, which was probably an apt description since they were the first settlers on the land. In 1811 they added another tract of 113 acres to the south.[62] Jacob farmed with his sons Jacob, Peter, and John. Between 1810 and 1820, there were a number of changes. In 1815 Peter and his wife, Catherine Winger, and their eight children decided to move to Tuscarawas County, Ohio. This may mean that Jacob and Barbara died a short while before, although we do not know their death dates. They are said to be buried on their farm, but there is no trace of graves left.

AAMG has noted that Jacob, Jr., was probably their oldest son, rather than John as it is in *DJH*, and a careful study of census records confirms this.[63] Jacob was married to Mary Schultz, a neighboring farmer's daughter. There were Schultzes in neighboring Greenville Township. In fact, the settlement of the Hochstetlers was in that direction, to the southwest, toward Pocahontas. Barbara and Jacob's youngest son John helped farm the family farm and became the eventual owner. His first wife was Elizabeth Hinckle, and they had four children. Elizabeth died fairly young. A bit later John married Elizabeth Stevanus, of a family that was not Amish, but a number of their children married and became Amish. John and his second wife had eight more children, most of whom remained in the area. It was this generation that joined the Church of the Brethren, also called Dunkers, and the parents were members as well.

In addition to farming, John was assessed as a distiller, not too uncommon on frontier farms. He was called Lame John according to the Hochstetler history, so he probably had some infirmity. The older brother, Jacob, who was also helping on the farm, seems to have had some serious disabilities. He had dropsy, was blind in the latter years of his life, and died rather young at the age of fifty-nine. His body had become so enlarged that they had to cut the door wider to allow his body to pass through. The middle brother, Peter, lived in Ohio between Sugarcreek and Ragersville in Tuscarawas County. Before that, Peter had a farm near his father's, which he sold to George Arnold. Some of Peter's children moved farther west to Indiana and other states, while others stayed in Ohio.[64]

Catherine, the only daughter of Barbara and Jacob, was married twice: first to Jacob Lint, then to George Klingaman, both prominent members of the German Baptist (Brethren) Church. From these two marriages the descendants spread into Greenville Township around Pocahontas. They formed a large part of what came to be called the Hostetler Church of the Brethren. Some of the children of Jacob and John Hochstetler, the brothers of Catherine, also contributed to this as they married into the Arnold, Bittinger, Bluebaugh, Klingaman, Lint, Livengood, Meyers, and Schultz families.[65]

The family boasts of one bishop or elder in the Church of the Brethren, Edwin Klingaman Hochstetler, who served the Hostetler Church of the Brethren near Pocahontas, where he is buried. He was the son of Jacob, Jr.'s son Samuel

---

[62] *DJH*.
[63] *AAMG* (section HS on Hochstetlers).
[64] *DJH*, #3 and following.
[65] *DJH*, #266.

and his second wife, Lydia Klingaman. She was the daughter of Jacob, Jr.'s sister Catherine and her husband, George Klingaman, and therefore, Samuel's first cousin. E.K., as he was affectionately called, was married to Mollie Slagle, daughter of Henry Slagle and Katherine Krider.[66]

The nearest Miller relative that Barbara and Jacob had in their area was Barbara's brother Peter, who lived just south and west of them along the Casselman River, also south of Meyersdale. Barbara's brother John lived several miles up the river beyond Meyersdale. Until 1800, this was all part of Elklick Township. Summit Township, north of the river, was part of Brothers Valley. At the present time, the original farm of Barbara and Jacob is at least partly owned by the Walker family. The city of Meyersdale is slowly enveloping it, though in the summer of 1997 it was still a going farm, with house and barn on opposite sides of the road, and cows were waiting to be milked. On all sides were signs of urban development. It is only a matter of time until the whole farm will be part of the city.

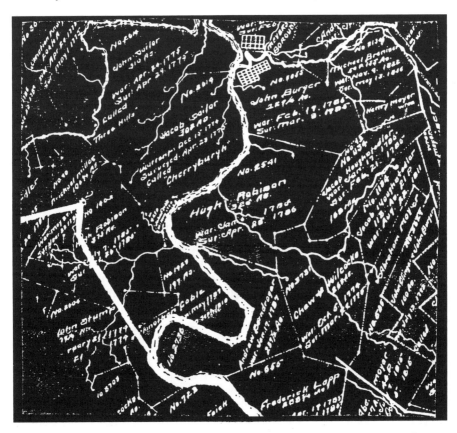

Plat map of part of Summit Township, Somerset County, Pennsylvania, showing original farms of Barbara Miller and Jacob Hochstetler southwest of Meyersdale, Pennsylvania.

---

[66] *DJH* #3-1386; *AAMG*, pp. 122-147.

Cemetery at the Hostetler Church of the Brethren showing the grave of Edwin Klingaman Hochstetler descendant of Barbara and Jacob, who became a bishop or elder in the Hostetler Church of the Brethren, Pocahontas, Greenville Township, Somerset County. DJH#266. Photo by J. Virgil Miller.

The Children of Barbara Miller and Jacob Hochstetler

1. **Jacob Hochstetler**, born 1778; died 1837; lived at Meyersdale, Pennsylvania; married Mary Schultz, born ca1777. Members of the Dunkard or German Baptist Brethren Church. They had four sons and six daughters.
2. **Peter Hochstetler**, born March 14, 1779; lived near Meyersdale, Pennsylvania; later moved to Tuscarawas County, Ohio; farmer; buried near Sugarcreek, Ohio. Married 1) Catherine Wingard, born ca1780; died ca1815. They had eight children, five sons and three daughters. He married 2) Margaret Alleshouse, widow of Mr. Horner. They had two sons and three daughters; he died July 21, 1841. Members of the Dunkard or German Baptist Church.
3. **Catherine Hochstetler**, born February 1, 1784; died June 11, 1867. She married George Klingaman, born September 30, 1798; died 1856. They had one son and eleven daughters.
4. **John Hochstetler**, born 1790; died March 15, 1854; lived at Meyersdale, Pennsylvania. Married 1) Elizabeth Hinckle; died before 1825. They had four children, two sons and two daughters. He m. 2) Elizabeth Stevanus, born ca1802. They had three sons and five daughters. He was a farmer and distiller. They were members of the Dunkard or German Baptist Church.

II. The Family of John Miller, Jr., and Freny Yoder

John Miller, Jr., was probably the oldest son of the eleven children of John Miller, Sr. He was born in Berks County about 1752, after his father had been in America about three years. At the time of the Indian troubles, he would have been only about three years old. After the French and Indian War, he and his two older brothers, Jacob and Peter, helped to clear land for farming. It is possible that the Miller sons helped on various farms in Upper Tulpehocken and Upper Bern Townships.

In the course of time John, or Hannes as he was called, was married to Freny Yoder, the daughter of Christian Yoder, also of the Northkill community. The Yoder farm was a bit further east in what is now Tilden Township, though it was formerly all Bern Township. There were several Yoder families. This Christian Yoder was the son of Jacob Yoder, an immigrant of 1742. Christian Yoder stayed in Berks County, although a number of his children migrated to Somerset County. Christian was a near neighbor of Benedict Lehman and Bishop Jacob Hertzler, who lived in Tilden Township near Hamburg, on the Schuylkill River. Two of Jacob Hertzler's sons married daughters of this Christian Yoder.

If we accept that Benedict Lehman's daughter Magdalena was married to John Miller, Sr., there is a reason for John Miller, Jr., to be married to Freny Yoder, for the Lehmans and the Yoders were near neighbors. Catherine Hertzler was married to John Hochstetler, the son of Immigrant Jacob. Jacob Yoder, son of Christian, was married to Freny, daughter of John Hochstetler. His brother, John Yoder, was married to Magdalena Stutzman, daughter of John Hochstetler's sister Barbara, married to Christian Stutzman. A daughter of the same Christian Yoder, Anna, was married to Jacob Stutzman, a son of Barbara Hochstetler Stutzman. This illustrates the complex family ties, until you can almost fill in the blanks. Geographical and blood connections continue within families that emphasize marriage within the religious group. See chart below.

John Miller, Jr., came to Somerset County about 1775 with his parents as a young married man. After some farming in connection with his Miller siblings in Elklick and Brothers Valley Townships, John, Jr., chose a tract of 111 1/2 acres at one of the bends of the Casselman River on the south side, about three miles northwest of Meyesrdale.[67] His near neighbors were Jacob and John Seiler (Saylor) and Christian and Johannes Gnagey, members of the Amish community. On the other side of the river lived his brother-in-law, John Yoder. A bit further north near Yoder's Station lived Freny's brother Jacob Yoder and his wife Freny Hochstetler, daughter of John. The whole community was called the River Church because it included everything south and along the Casselman River, including Elklick Township. The first minister of this group apparently was John Miller, Jr.'s brother Jacob, known as Yockel, who lived further away near Springs in Elklick Township. Until about 1800 the whole area south of the river was Elklick Township and north of it was Brothers Valley. Later, a township was formed from land on both sides of the river, with Meyersdale as the chief town, and the new township was called Summit. So before 1800 the River Church covered a fairly large area. The church or *Gemeinde* (Amish— *Gmee*) was a fellowship that got together, if possible, every two weeks.[68]

John and Freny's oldest son, Yost, was born in 1776 and came to Somerset County with them. He was married about 1800 to Gertraut Yoder, daughter of another Christian Yoder, who was married to Barbara Holly and lived in the Glades in Stony Creek Township. This Christian was a cousin of the father of Freny, wife of John, Jr. Yost Miller obtained a tract of land in 1802 from John Geeting, of 302 acres, which he held until 1815 when he sold it to Abraham Miller, the son of John, Jr.'s brother, Peter. Then Yost and his wife moved to Holmes County, Ohio, where he was a pioneer in Walnut Creek Township. It is stated erroneously in the Hochstetler history that John, Jr., also moved to Ohio in 1815, but this is impossible, because his will is in the Somerset County Courthouse, stating that he died in 1802.[69] John, Jr.'s, estate was administered by his sons Yost and David, ages twenty-six and twenty-three. It is possible that John, Jr., intended to move to Ohio and that he was a member of a party to investigate settlement possibilities, but died before the migration took place. John's brother Jacob had already gone to Tuscarawas County, Ohio, in 1809.[70]

John, Jr., like his father Hannes, Sr., had a total of eleven children. Whereas the eleven offspring of John, Sr., all grew up to produce families, the youngest two of John, Jr., died young. They all moved to Holmes County, Ohio, without exception. The children who raised families all married into families with Amish-Mennonite names, nine in all. Four married Yoders, three married Troyers, one married a Hochstetler, two married Beachys, and one married a Gnagey. Some of course, were second or even third marriages.[71] When John Miller, Jr., died in 1802, his farm was also sold to Abraham Miller, son of his brother Peter. Abraham was married to Mary, daughter of John, Jr.'s, neighbor, John Saylor. Abraham and Mary are buried on this farm. There are no remaining stones marking the graves of Hannes, Jr., and wife Freny, but it is almost certain that they are buried there, according to family custom.

---

[67] Land records, Somerset Co., and Summit Twp. plat map. Refers to him as Hannes Miller, Jr.

[68] Information in various histories of Amish and Mennonites.

[69] From Moses B. Miller, Appendix to *DJH* #1946 ff. and *AAMG*. Information about the supposed move to Ohio is p. 955 (*DJH*).

[70] Actual death date from will of Jacob Miller, 1801, Somerset Courthouse.

[71] From my own research and *AAMG*.

Interrelationship of Northkill Amish-Mennonites

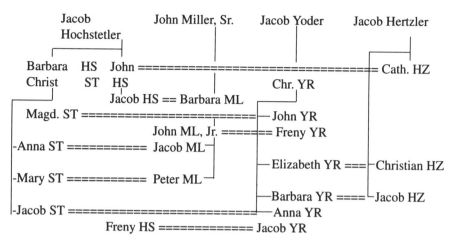

A diagram showing the close inter-relationships of the Northkill Amish-Mennonite Community in the eighteenth century.

The Children of John Miller, Jr., and Freny Yoder

1. **Yost Miller**, born 1776, Berks County, Pennsylvania; came to Holmes County with his parents; lived in Somerset County until 1816; married 1) Gertraut Yoder, born 1778. They moved then to Holmes County, Ohio, where they were pioneers. She died in 1830; he died in 1846. He m. 2) Marie Follmer (1783-1846). He was a farmer; also acted as a community leader, helping people with their legal problems. They had eleven children, only four of whom married and had families; three sons and two daughters grew to maturity; one daughter was single; Amish.
2. **Daniel Miller**, born 1778; died 1858; married 1) Magdalena Troyer, born in Somerset County; died in Holmes County, Ohio. He married 2) Magdalena Miller, born 1803; death date not known. In first marriage had seven sons and three daughters; no children from second marriage. They lived in Holmes County, Ohio; Amish.
3. **David Miller**, born 1779; died 1840; married Elizabeth Troyer, born 1781; death date unknown. He was a farmer and lived in Holmes County, Ohio. They had fourteen sons and one daughter; three sons died young; Amish.
4. **Catherine Miller**, born 1783; died 1842; married Benjamin Hochstetler, born 1782; died 1853. They lived in Tuscarawas County, Ohio; he was a farmer. They had four sons and eight daughters; Amish.
5. **Jacob Miller**, born 1784; died 1830; married Freny Troyer, born 1779; death date unknown. Moved to Holmes County, Ohio; farmer. They had three sons and six daughters; Amish.

6. **John Miller**, born 1787; died 1867; married Anna Gnagey, born 1787; died 1872. He was a farmer and lived in Holmes County, Ohio; Amish. They had four sons and five daughters.
7. **Elizabeth Miller**, born 1789; died 1841; married Moses Beachey, born 1790; died 1840. He was a bishop in the Amish-Mennonite church; also a farmer. They had five sons and seven daughters. Two of their sons were bishops in the Old Order Amish (Moses) and the Amish-Mennonite (David) Churches.
8. **Isaac Miller**, born 1791; died 1871; married 1) Mary Yoder, born 1791; died 1817. They had two sons and one daughter. He married 2) Sarah Beachy, and had three sons and three daughters. He married 3) Mary Mosser, born 1801; died 1889. They had three daughters. They lived in Holmes County, Ohio, and belonged to the Amish Church; farmer.
9. **Emanuel Miller**, born 1792; died 1848; married Elizabeth Yoder, born 1793; death date unknown. They lived in Holmes County, Ohio. They had four sons and five daughters; farmer; Amish.
10. **Solomon Miller**, born 1795; died young in accident while cutting timber; moved to Holmes County, Ohio.
11. **Elias Miller**, born 1798; died single.

This family was composed of eleven children, like that of John, Sr., except that the last two died single. It was unusual in that all of them moved to Ohio and stayed with the Amish-Mennonite Church. They had ninety-seven grandchildren who raised families.[72]

The homestead of John Miller, Jr., in Summit Township, Somerset County, Pennsylvania. The house is now owned by the Kinsinger family. Photo by J. Virgil Miller.

---

[72] *Miller Family History.* AAMG.

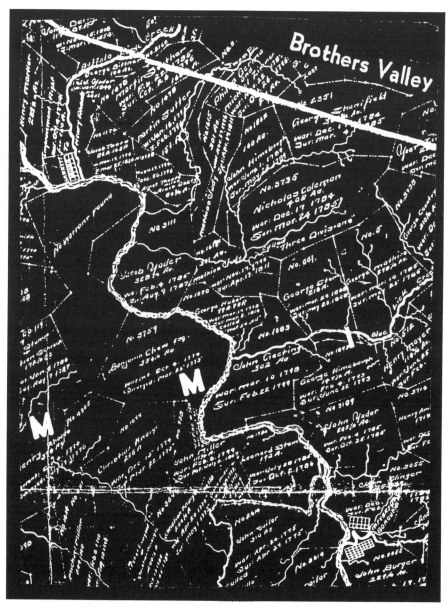

Part of the plat map of Summit Township, Somerset County, Pennsylvania, showing the homesteads of Jacob Yoder, John Miller, Jr., John Yoder, Yost Miller, and John Geeting.

Picture of Daniel B. Miller (1838-1928), the writer's great-grandfather, of Walnut Creek, Holmes County, Ohio. He was the grandson of Yost Miller, the pioneer of Holmes County, Ohio. His father was Benjamin Miller.

Farm cemetery showing the tombstones of Yost Miller, son of John Miller, Jr., east of Walnut Creek, Ohio. The stones leaning against the tree are of Yost and his second wife, Marie Follmer. Holmes County, Ohio. Photo by J. Virgil Miller.

III. The Family of Jacob Miller and Anna Stutzman

Jacob Miller was the third child, second son of John (Hannes) Miller, Sr. He was born in Berks County, Pennsylvania, in 1754. As a young man he accompanied his father to Bedford County to the part that is now Elklick Township, Somerset County. In those days the family acted as a unit. It is not quite clear when the whole family moved to Somerset County. We see John Miller taxed in Berks County and Somerset County at the same time. Probably when Jacob was courting Anna Stutzman about 1775 it was Berks County, since Barbara Stutzman, the mother, did not move to Somerset County at all.[73] Perhaps when the rest of the family was beginning to till the farm their father had bought in Elklick Township in 1775, Jacob and his brother Peter were helping Widow Barbara Stutzman to take care of her farm, since her sons were still young. John, the father, had some crops to take care of before they could move; besides, the first children were being born.

All this has to be left for the imagination to tell the sequence of events. When John and Anna and their children finally came to Somerset County to live, local tradition says that he first lived in the Glades. If this is true, then Jacob must have cultivated the tract that his father had been paying for since 1771.[74] As related elsewhere, the tracts that the first settlers selected were not always the places where they finally settled. In some cases an entirely different person took over the warrant because the original warrantee decided not to move across the mountains. In the case of the Millers, they simply held on to the land until some family member wished to cultivate it. As related in the previous section, Hannes Miller, the father, was thinking of settling in Elklick Township near some friends from Berks County. When Jacob and Anna came along after the death of Barbara Stutzman, they began in the Glades, no doubt assisted by other family members.[75]

---

[73] Rev. Harvey Hostetler, *Descendants of Barbara Hochstedler and Christian Stutzman (DBH)* (Berlin, Ohio: Gospel Book Store, 1988), p. 6.
[74] *Pennsylvania Archives*, tax records, Bedford Co., 1771.
[75] *The Joel B. Miller History*, p. 20.

Homestead of Jacob Miller, son of John Miller, Sr., in Elklick Township, Somerset County, Pennsylvania, before moving to Tuscarawas County, Ohio, in 1809. It is known locally as "the Sam Davis place." Photo by J. Virgil Miller.

After 1790, or perhaps even before, Jacob had his own farm in Elklick Township, located northwest of Springs on what was called the Sam Davis place at the foot of Negro Mountain. By this time they had four sons: John, Benedict, Henry, and Jacob, Jr. Jacob was apparently interested in land investment. The Elklick Township farm was only one of his warrants. He also took out warrants across the border in Maryland. It is doubtful whether he ever lived in Maryland, but there was considerable acreage, and the tract he bought in 1798 was said to be 300 acres. [76] In 1814 a resurvey showed that the tract was actually 353 acres. The farm near Springs was transferred to Jacob's son Benedict in 1808. [77]

The following year Jacob decided to move to Ohio. He, with his wife Anna and his younger sons Henry and Jacob, took up land in Sugarcreek Township, Tuscarawas County, Ohio. [78] They made the trip by Conestoga wagon. Jacob had been the Amish-Mennonite minister and bishop in the Casselman River congregation in Elklick Township, and as other settlers came in, was the first minister in Ohio as well. They called him Yockel Miller and he at first served the Amish settlers in both Tuscarawas and Holmes Counties. Later he was associated with his son Jacob, Jr., in the ministry, and they served only in the Sugarcreek area in Tuscarawas County. His wife Anna died in 1814 and gradually

---

[76] *Ibid.*, p. 38.
[77] *Ibid.*, p. 39.
[78] *DJH*, p. 954.

The homestead of Jacob Miller, son of John Miller, Sr., in Tuscarawas County, Ohio, is located north of Sugarcreek, in Sugarcreek Township. It is now owned by Darrell Miller. Notice the cemetery in the foreground. Photos by J. Virgil Miller.

the duties of the ministry and the farm were given over to his son, Jacob, Jr. Jacob Miller died in 1835 at age eighty-one. Jacob and Anna are buried in a farm cemetery on their farm a few miles north of Sugarcreek. Their grave markers are no longer there, but those of Jacob, Jr., are still to be seen. Leroy Beachy, in his Amish cemetery book, has a plan of this historic cemetery showing the probable location of their graves. [79] The present owner of part of the original homestead is Darrell Miller.

---

[79] Leroy Beachy, *Cemetery Directory of the Amish Community in Eastern Holmes and Adjoining Counties in Ohio* (1975), p. 113.

The Children of Jacob Miller and Anna Stutzman

1. **John J. Miller**, born 1778; died 1861, Berks County, Pennsylvania. Came to Somerset County with his parents about 1783; lived in the Glades on the Miller homestead for a while and accompanied his parents to their farm in Elklick Township where they settled about 1790, when John would have been twelve. In 1798 when his father Jacob was acquiring land in the Mt. Nebo area of nearby Maryland, John would have been twenty years old. A year or so after that, John was married to Anna Gnagey, daughter of Christian Gnagey. It is possible that John then lived at his father's Mt. Nebo land in Maryland. Two children were born to John and his first wife: daughters Rachel and Anna. After Anna's birth about 1805, John married a second wife, Catherine. Some think she was Catherine, the daughter of John Hochstetler. *AAMG* leaves it blank. They had four sons and two daughters, all born in Tuscarawas County, Ohio, where they moved in 1810. John added the initial "J" to his name and became John J. Miller. He was a farmer and mill operator in Ohio, and lived at Barrs Mills in Tuscarawas County. After the first Catherine died in 1822, he married Catherine Willard. They had two sons and a daughter. About 1850 they moved to near Kokomo, Indiana, where he died.[80]

John J. Miller was one of the few Amish-Mennonites to have his picture taken. This photo taken around 1860 is from The Miller Story.

---

[80] See *DJH* #9148. *DBH* #3313. Notations from the John J. Miller family Bible.

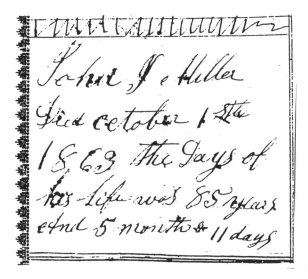

Notice of the death of John J. Miller taken from his family Bible.

2. **Benedict Miller**, born 1781, Berks County, Pennsylvania; died 1837; married 1) Catherine Beachy, born 1778; died 1834. He came with his parents to Somerset County, Pennsylvania, where they lived in the Glades area for several years. After his father bought his Elklick Township farm, he helped his father on the farm until 1808, when Jacob decided to move to Ohio. This coincided with the choice by lot of Benedict to be the minister of the Casselman River congregation. Benedict felt it was the call of God so he decided to stay, even though all the other members of Jacob's family moved to Ohio. Benedict continued to operate the Elklick Township farm, which is called the Sam Davis farm locally. In 1821 Peter Bitsche (Beachy), his father-in-law, deeded over to Benedict and Catherine the Bitsche-Beachy homestead near Springs and the Maryland border. They lived there for the rest of their lives. After Catherine died in 1834, Benedict married Catherine Eash Keim, widow of Nicholas Keim. He lived only a few years after that, but he had two daughters from the second marriage. In the first marriage Benedict and Catherine had six sons and six daughters. After Benedict's death his son, Joel B. Miller, became the minister and bishop.[81]

3. **Henry Miller** was born in 1773; died 1868. He was married to Barbara Seese, born 1784; died 1854. Henry moved with his parents to Somerset County, then moved with his parents to Ohio in 1809 when he was already married. He obtained a tract of land just west of that of his father and brother, Jacob, Jr., in Tuscarawas County. When his father died, Henry was made the executor. There was quite a controversy about the inheritance. Henry apparently felt that he had not received his rightful share; it seemed to be about the land that Jacob had acquired in Maryland. Sons John and Benedict were involved in it, but the younger sons were not. Benedict died two years after his father, so

---

[81] *DBH*, #3450, ff. *AAMG*.

the matter became even more complicated. Henry became further estranged when he became a fervent member of the United Brethren, participating in their charismatic activities.[82] Henry and Barbara had twelve children, seven daughters and five sons. They lived on the quarter-section just west of his father and brother.

4. **Jacob Miller, Jr.**, born in Somerset County, moved to Ohio with his parents, and lived with his wife Dorothy Seese and children at his father's homestead, which they farmed jointly. He was born 1787; died 1852. She was born 1792 and died 1879. He succeeded his father Jacob as the minister and bishop of the Amish-Mennonite church in Tuscarawas County, Ohio.[83] They had two sons and seven daughters.

The inheritance question affects many families, but perhaps in this one it was caused first by the distance they had from each other, with Benedict in Pennsylvania. Some of the land in question was not in Ohio, and the executor, Henry Miller, belonged to another religious group. *AAMG* mentions two daughters besides the four sons, but with no names. Upon inquiry of local historians, I gathered that there was never any mention of daughters in the question of the inheritance. Two of the daughters were from the family of George Seese, a neighbor in Somerset County. On the plat map he is called George Sweet, an interesting translation of German "Süss," the original German form, but in English the name Süss became Seese.[84] George Seese or Sweet was not an Amish-Mennonite, but he had a number of daughters. I think the historians of *AAMG* noted in the census records that there were two parents, four males under twenty-one, and two females under twenty-one, and assumed there were two previously unknown daughters.

The answer seems to be that the family, having four sons, needed help in the kitchen, and hired two of the Seese girls. In the time-honored tradition of farm people everywhere, and especially among traditional people like the Amish and Mennonites, the boys in the family married the hired girls. Even before they were married, the census would count them as members of the household.[85]

---

[82] David I. Miller, "The State of Jacob's Estate," *The Historian*, Apr. 1991.
[83] See *AAMG*, #ML234, p. 278.
[84] Plat map of Elklick Twp.
[85] *AAMG*, p. 272.

IV. The Family of Peter Miller and Mary Stutzman

    Peter Miller was the third son of John Miller, Sr., born in Berks County, Pennsylvania, in 1756. He grew up on his father's farm. In 1776 at the age of nineteen, he moved with his parents to Somerset County. Their neighbors across the Northkill Creek in Berks County were the Stutzmans, and there must have been an understanding that Peter would come back and marry Mary Stutzman, one of the daughters, who was the sister of Anna, wife of Peter's brother Jacob. Or, possibly Peter stayed behind helping at the Stutzman farm, as Barbara had been a widow since 1770 and her older children were all girls.

    In the 1790 census, both Peter and his brother Jacob are listed in the census list for Bedford (now Somerset) County. By that time their father, John, Sr., had moved to his farm in Brothers Valley Township in the Glades, and had sold his Elklick Township farm to Peter Livengood who, interestingly, is listed in the census just next to the two brothers. Were they working for Livengood before taking over their own farms? By 1800 Peter and his wife Mary Stutzman were living near Meyersdale on what was to become their homestead. They had bought a farm from Hugh Robinson just south of Meyersdale on the east side of the Casselman River at the first bend of the river.[86]

    There is a stream flowing through it which is still called Miller's Run. Here they raised a family of six sons and three daughters, all of whom had families. The children were caught up in the move to Ohio. Jonas with his wife Catherine Hershberger; Magdalena with her husband John Troyer; and Sarah, wife of Joseph Mast, were three of the first four Amish couples to settle in Holmes County, Ohio, in 1810. They were joined later by Peter and Mary's youngest son, Moses, who became a prominent Amish-Mennonite minister in Ohio.[87]

    Peter Miller's children who stayed in Pennsylvania followed a different course. His oldest son Abraham took over the farm of his uncle, John Miller, Jr. The second son, Peter P. Miller, bought the farm of Andrew Bontrager, just south of the Peter Miller homestead at the next bend in the river. Consequently, Millers owned a considerable part of the land along the east bank of the river, if you

---

[86] Census, Bedford Co., Pa., 1790. See also plat map of Summit Twp.
[87] "History of Holmes Co., Ohio, settlement," *The Mennonite Encyclopedia*.

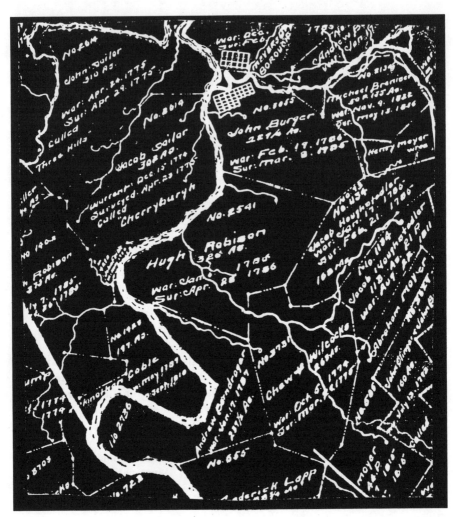

Part of the plat map of Summit Township, Somerset County, Pennsylvania, showing the farms of Peter Miller (Hugh Robinson farm) and of Peter P. Miller, his son (Andrew Bontrager farm). The Barbara Miller and Jacob Hochstetler farm is to the right. The area is south of Meyersdale, Pennsylvania.

count the farm of John, Jr., bought by Peter's son Abraham. Today the Peter Miller farm is completely gone, taken over by the city of Meyersdale. A large school grounds covers much of the area. The property was last owned by the Bowman family. The homestead of Peter and Mary, if my informants are correct, is still occupied by Bill Bowman. [88] It is in a housing development, and one house looking much like the others, is a log house with white clapboarding. Like the John Miller, Sr., house, the inside, and especially the attic and basement, show

---

[88] See picture.

The homestead of Peter Miller is now in an urban area of Meyersdale, Pennsylvania, near the Casselman River. Pictured are Mr. and Mrs. William Bowman with Dr. Alta Schrock. They were the last family to own the farm. Picture is as it is now. Photo by J. Virgil Miller.

the log construction. Mr. Bowman said there had been a fire, causing them to take off part of the upper story, but the house remains. If this isn't Peter's house, it is certainly an old one, probably on the same site.

After Peter's death the farm was apparently taken over by one of his sons, probably Joseph. In 1875 when the atlas of Somerset County was made, there was still a Miller on Peter's farm: Samuel J. Miller, the son of Abraham's son, John A. Miller. The farm of Peter Miller, Jr., has been in the family up to the present. In 1875, at the time of the atlas, it was owned by Samuel P. Miller, the son of Peter P. Miller,[89] the same as Peter Miller, Jr. Samuel's descendants still live there.

Peter and Mary were formerly buried on their farm in a farm cemetery, as reported in the cemetery guide of Somerset County. According to that guide, Peter and his wife had stones marked "PM 1818" and "MM March 23, 1838." Also mentioned was one of Daniel Gnagey's children, a Mrs. Hostetler[90] (could it be Peter's sister Barbara?), and Mrs. Samuel R. Fike. The Fikes were neighbors and the Gnageys lived not far away, but all the stones were reported to have been moved to the Union Cemetery in Meyersdale, but the stones cannot be found.

Peter's estate papers are in the Somerset County Courthouse. He left the farm to his son Joseph, to whom he gave an extra 450 pounds to take care of Peter's widow, Mary. She was to get twenty-eight pounds yearly.[91] As it happened Mary lived twenty years after him.

---

[89] F. W. Beers, *County Atlas of Somerset, Pennsylvania* (New York: 1876).
[90] *Cemetery Guide*, in Somerset Public Library.
[91] Estate settlement of Peter Miller, in records in Somerset Co. Courthouse.

The homestead of Peter P. Miller now owned by Mr. Long and Corey Miller, descendants of Peter P. Miller, is located south of Meyersdale, Pennsylvania. Photo by J. Virgil Miller.

It is interesting to note the church affiliation of the Peter Miller family. Those who stayed near the family homestead remained Amish for at least one generation. Sons Peter and Joseph were Amish, but Joseph's children joined the Church of the Brethren, which was strong around Meyersdale. Peter, Jr.,'s children remained Amish for several more generations, but eventually his son, Samuel P. Miller, who inherited the Peter P. Miller farm, married Susanna Klingaman and joined the Brethren. His son Samuel S. Miller, his grandson Howard Miller, and Howard's son and daughter, Ernest and Corrie Miller, have owned the farm up to the present.[92] My wife and I turned off the 219 Highway to follow a sign marked "Maple Syrup," and were pleased to find the Peter P. Miller farm. Mr. Long, the husband of Corey Miller, sold us the syrup.

The children of Peter Miller and Mary Stutzman who moved westward tended to stay with the Amish. Magdalena and Sarah were pioneers in Holmes County, Ohio. Jeremiah married Elizabeth Livengood and moved to Pulaski, Iowa, to a community of new immigrants from Europe. Their daughter Mary was married to Christian Brenneman, who came from Waldeck, Germany, via Somerset County. Their son Jeremiah, Jr., was married to Elizabeth Schwarzendrover, also from Germany.[93] So the family expanded, both geographically and ethnically, but many were active in the Amish and Mennonite churches.

---

[92] Somerset Co. land records.
[93] Anne Augspurger Schmidt-Lange, "Descendants of Jeremiah Miller of Somerset County," *MFH*, Jan. 1998.

The Children of Peter Miller and Mary Stutzman

1. **Abraham Miller**, born 1780; died 1849; married Mary Saylor, born 1780; died 1846. They lived north of Meyersdale, Pennsylvania, and belonged to the Church of the Brethren. They had seven sons and five daughters.
2. **Magdalena Miller**, born 1781; died ca1820; married John Troyer, born ca1781; died 1813. They moved near Walnut Creek, Ohio, in 1810, where he died a few years later as a relatively young man. They had three sons and two daughters. Amish-Mennonite.
3. **Peter P. Miller**, born 1783; died 1852; married Barbara Yoder, born 1785; died 1850. They lived near Meyersdale, Pennsylvania. He was a farmer. They had seven sons and six daughters who raised families; two daughters died young. Amish-Mennonite.
4. **Jonas Miller**, born 1788, died 1854; married Catherine Hershberger, born 1789; died 1869. They moved to Holmes County, Ohio, and lived near Walnut Creek. Amish-Mennonite. They had four sons and six daughters; two children died single. One son, Moses J. Miller, also called Klein Mose or Glee Mose (Little Mose) was a leading minister in the formation of the Old Order Amish.
5. **Joseph Miller**, born 1790; died 1862; married Catherine Livengood, born 1798; died 1871. They lived near Meyersdale, Pennsylvania. Amish-Mennonite. They had five sons and seven daughters.
6. **Jeremiah Miller**, born 1790; died 1868; married Elizabeth Livengood, born April 13, 1788; died 1861. They moved near Pulaski, Iowa. They had two children, Mary and Jeremiah. Mary married Christian Brenneman, born in Waldeck, Germany; Jeremiah married Anna Schlatter.
7. **Sarah Miller**, born 1794; died 1847; married Joseph Mast, born 1786; died 1850. They lived near Walnut Creek, Ohio. Amish-Mennonite. They had three sons and five daughters.
8. **Mary Miller**, born 1798; died 1847; married Peter Livengood, born 1791; died 1861. They had three sons and four daughters; a son and a daughter died young. They lived near Meyersdale, Pennsylvania. Amish-Mennonite. He married 2) Catherine Eash, widow of Nicholas Keim and Benedict Miller. She was the third wife of Keim, the second wife of Benedict. When Peter Livengood died, she moved to Holmes County, Ohio, with her five Keim children and two Miller children. She was born in 1799 and died 1889.
9. **Moses P. Miller**, born 1802; died 1877; married Catherine Miller, daughter of Broad Run John Miller, born 1795; died 1871. They lived near Walnut Creek, Ohio, and had four sons and one daughter; three daughters died young. He was a bishop in the Amish-Mennonite Church, which erected church buildings and gradually merged with the Mennonite Church. He was one of their leaders.

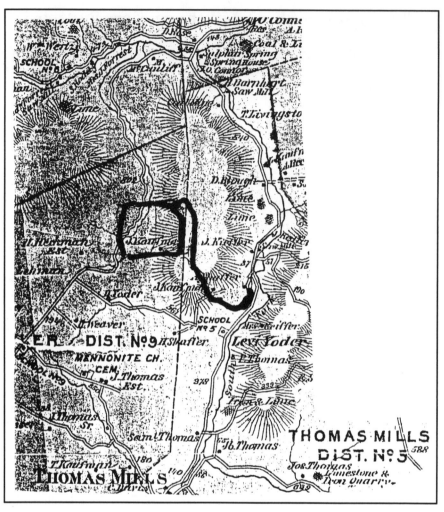

This map shows the general location of the Kauffman farms in the western part of Conemaugh Township, Somerset County. Note the approximate location of the homestead and the Kauffman Road.

V. The Family of Catherine Miller and Jacob Kauffman

Catherine was probably the second daughter of John Miller, Sr. The study of the ages of the children of Jacob Kauffman makes it clear that either Catherine was a second wife, or she was older than some records say she was. Thus she could be older. That is what *AAMG* concludes, making her born ca1758, which would make her older than either Christian or Joseph. There is an additional problem, because there were two Jacob Kauffmans living in Conemaugh Township at the same time, and both were married to a Catherine Miller.

The younger Catherine, born in 1773, was the one married to Jacob Kauffman as his second wife, but it was the other Jacob. I am eternally grateful to the authors of *AAMG* for showing this. Thus we can accept Catherine, the daughter of John Miller, Sr., as the mother of all Jacob Kauffman's children if her date of birth is set at about 1758.[94] The two Jacobs can be separated geographically as well as genealogically. There is the Jacob of the eastern part of Conemaugh, and the Jacob of the west in the area between Thomas Mills and the North Fork area. This also agrees with the location of Catherine's siblings in Jenner Township and in Conemaugh, between Jerome and Thomas Mills.[95]

The 1875 atlas map of Conemaugh Township shows a J. Kauffman living north of Thomas Mennonite Church, about three miles. Using the cue that the gravestone of Catherine's brother "Glades" Christian seems to be in the oldest part of the Thomas Cemetery, I looked farther and made inquiries after attending church there, and found that the oldest part of the cemetery was older than the first church building. That showed me that it was originally an Amish cemetery. There were a number of Kauffmans among the older graves which a descendant told me were grandsons of Jacob Kauffman.[96]

Using the old 1875 atlas as a guide, we drove up toward the North Fork Dam. At the road turning right about three or four miles north of the Thomas Church we turned, and for an hour or so we wound over the hills and around the

---

[94] *AAMG*, p. 163.
[95] See map of the area on page 50 (from 1875 atlas).
[96] See map of area.

A marker showing the "Top Kauffman Street." Further along the same road is the Owen Lehman farm. Photo by J. Virgil Miller.

curves in a scenic hilly area until we came to what seemed the end of the road. I finally asked a lady living in an attractive newer home, obviously not a farm house, if she knew what families formerly lived in the area.

"Well," she said, "my husband is descended from the Keims." The name was familiar. [97] And back several miles is a sign that says "Upper Kauffman Hill Road."

My wife and I drove back several miles, saw the sign but no houses nearby. Near the beginning of the road where we had turned off, I saw a traditional-looking farm in the valley.

I said, "If that isn't Jacob and Catherine Kauffman's homestead, it ought to be!" [98]

The house was very traditional, having a wide veranda, with many rooms. Surprisingly, the owner was related to a friend of ours. His name was Owen Lehman, and his wife was an Eash. This was the Sem K. Eash farm. We talked animatedly. Though interested, Owen knew little of the history of the place. He vaguely remembered that the road used to be called Kauffman Road; why, he didn't know.

When I got back to the Somerset County Courthouse, I decided to trace the Lehman farm in the deed records. After going through a long line of Eashes, I finally found the name of Jonas Kauffman. It was the next to youngest son of Jacob and Catherine (west side). I knew the "other" Jacob Kauffman lived near Davidsville in the east of Conemaugh, and this was west, and this Jacob had a Jonas. I couldn't trace farther. I could just imagine a whole line of Kauffmans from the Lehman farm to the Upper Kauffman Hill Road. I failed to go further.

Catherine and Jacob must have been married about 1780, and this is the only reason for suggesting 1758 as her birth date. Since the other Jacob

---

[97] *Ibid.*
[98] See picture on page 53.

The Owen Lehman farm on the old Kauffman Road, north of Thomas Mills, Conemaugh Township, Somerset County, Pennsylvania. Once the farm of Jonas Kauffman, son of Jacob Kauffman and Catherine Miller. Possibly the farm of the parents. Photo by J. Virgil Miller.

Kauffman's wife, Catherine Miller, was a second wife, it is only natural to conclude that she was the one born in 1772, as given on a number of records. The will of the western Jacob Kauffman has been located in the Somerset Courthouse, dated 1825.[99] His wife's name is given as Maria, so we may assume that she was a second wife of his relatively old age. Nothing is given of the date of Catherine's death, but it must have been between the birth of Moses, her youngest child, and 1825, the date of Jacob's estate settlement. Jacob's will, or more correctly, his estate settlement, was signed by his executors, John Mittenberger and Daniel Hershberger. Daniel's daughter Anna was married to Jacob Kauffman, the oldest son of the deceased Jacob. Daniel may have been a near neighbor and fellow church member who was familiar with the administration of estate settlements.

Jacob willed, among other bequests, a third of his property to his widow Mary, in addition to her spinning wheel, a stove and chest, and the clock. Besides some farm items, he wills her a saddle, one cow, one heifer, and fifty dollars in money to be paid out of the estate. To his youngest sons, Jonas and Moses, who were about twenty-three and twenty-one years old and not married, he gave one horse and one bed each. The remainder was to be equally divided with the other heirs. Christian's share was to be kept by Jacob's son John, to be kept for Christian until the end of his life. This must indicate that Christian had left home and they did not know where he was at the time. We have no record at all about him except that he was a son.

---

[99] Will of Jacob Kauffman, 1825. Somerset Co. Courthouse.

Debts owed to the estate included one account on Solomon, one of the younger sons, who may have borrowed money to set up farming. There was a debt of $23.29; another was by the Widow Berkey, which must have referred to his daughter married to David Berkey, who had died in about 1821. That amount was $67.29. John Kauffman, one of the sons, had a debt of $27.80. Those amounts were to be subtracted from their share of the estate. The total amount from the sale and the debts to be paid amounted to $716, a sizable amount. However, with thirteen children and a widow the share may seem small, but in those days actual money in hand was considerably less.

One interesting item in the will that might establish that this is the right Jacob Kauffman married to Catherine Miller is from Joseph Miller of Elklick Township to Moses Kauffman, for the use of the Jacob Kauffman estate. It is a small amount, $5.90.[100] Joseph must have been the son of Peter Miller who lived near Meyersdale and, therefore, the cousin of Moses Kauffman. We can picture him, as the youngest son, working in Elklick Township for his cousin, and the question of this small debt came up. This shows there was a special relationship of some kind for Moses to go that far to work.

It had something to do with the estate of John Troyer, who died early as one of the pioneers in Holmes County, Ohio. Perhaps Moses Kauffman worked for the Troyers as well at one time. Nevertheless, my doubts about Catherine's identity have become less as I read this item. One could ask why Isaac Lehman and John Kauffman were administrators of the estate of Jacob Kauffman at this stage. Another observation is that Isaac Lehman, a farmer in Conemaugh Township in the western part, was the son of John Lehman and a wife named Mary ___; the record in *AAMG* is blank. Could Mary ___ have married Jacob Kauffman as a widow in his old age? That would make Isaac and John stepbrothers. But there must not be too much speculation—I am only raising the question. The Miller connection seems firm in spite of the absence of Catherine's name in the will. The thirteen children are then named in the will.

The Children of Catherine Miller and Jacob Kauffman

1. **John Kauffman**, born 1781; died 1855; married to Freny Hershberger. They lived in Conemaugh Township, Somerset County, Pennsylvania. He was a farmer and lived near his parents. He had six children, three sons and three daughters. Amish-Mennonite Church. His children all stayed with the Amish Church and lived in Conemaugh Township.
2. **Christian Kauffman**, born ca1782. His address was unknown in 1825 at the time his father made his will. A provision of the will was that Christian's share should be kept for him by the oldest son, John, until the end of his life. It is not known if there was an estrangement and that Christian had left home, but there is no indication that he was in disfavor with the family. There is no further knowledge of Christian.

---

[100] *Ibid.*

3. **Barbara Kauffman**, born ca1784; married David Berkey, who died some time before 1825 since Barbara was a widow at the time of her father's death. They were living in Conemaugh Township in 1810. They were probably Amish and had nine children, five sons and four daughters.
4. **Magdalena Kauffman**, born 1785; died 1862; married Jonathan Miller, born 1789; died 1867. He was the son of Bishop Christian "Schmidt" Miller, who came to Conemaugh Township in 1780 and lived near Jerome. Magdalena and Jonathan moved to Holmes County, Ohio, and lived near Charm, where Magdalena died and is buried. Jonathan went on to become a pioneer in Lagrange County, Indiana. He moved there with his son Joni and lived with him until he died. Magdalena and Jonathan had five sons and seven daughters; the first seven children were girls.
5. **Elizabeth Kauffman**, born ca1787; married John Garver, born ca1786; died 1865. He was born in Cumru Township, Berks County, Pennsylvania, then moved to Conemaugh Township, Somerset County, where he married Elizabeth. They moved to Holmes County, Ohio, with several of their children, and finally to Elkhart County, Indiana. They had eight daughters and one son, scattered from Ohio to Indiana, Iowa, and Kansas.
6. **Maria Kauffman**, born 1789; died 1861; married John Thomas, born 1796; died 1876. They lived and died in Conemaugh Township. John was the brother of Jacob Thomas, who married the daughter of "Glades" Christian Miller, brother of Catherine, mother of Maria of this family. Jacob Thomas's second wife, Rachel Miltenberger, was the daughter of John Miltenberger, one of Jacob Kauffman's executors. Maria and John Thomas stayed in Somerset County and are probably buried in the Thomas Mennonite Church Cemetery. They had four sons and five daughters.
7. **Gertrude Kauffman**, born ca1791; died 1847; married Peter Yoder, born 1773; died 1849, as his second wife. He was born in Mifflin County, Pennsylvania, where he was married to Freny Kauffman and had six children before she died in 1817. After Peter Yoder's marriage to Gertrude, they moved first to Wayne County, and then to Logan County, Ohio. There were five sons and three daughters from the second marriage. They belonged to the Amish-Mennonite Church.
8. **Jacob Kauffman**, born 1793; died 1859; married Rebecca Plank, born 1801; died 1873; They moved to Holmes County, Ohio, and later to Johnson County, Iowa. They had fifteen children, twelve of whom raised families. Of these, there were nine sons and three daughters. Amish-Mennonite Church.
9. **Solomon Kauffman**, born 1796; died 1881; married Magdalena Hostetler, born 1796; died 1877. They lived in Conemaugh Township, Somerset County. They had six sons and five daughters. Amish-Mennonite Church.
10. **Abraham Kauffman**, born ca1798; died __; married Susanna Keck, born 1805; died 1881; They moved to Holmes County, Ohio, where they died. They had five sons and three daughters.
11. **Freny Kauffman**, born 1800; died 1877; married Christian Yoder, born 1787; died 1867 as his second wife. He had been married to Judith Gindelsberger,

who bore him ten children; she died in 1832. Freny and Christian had a son and a daughter. They lived in Stony Creek Township, Somerset County, Pennsylvania.

12. **Jonas Kauffman**, born ca1802; died ca1870; married 1) Freny Keim, born ca1815; died after 1850. He m. 2) Magdalena Miller, born 1826; died 1892. Some time after 1870 they moved to Kent County, Michigan. In Jonas's first marriage he had thirteen children, eleven of whom married and had families; one son died in the army and another child died in infancy. In the second marriage, they had five children, but only two grew up to have families. No children reported. Some of the children of the first marriage also moved with their family to Michigan, but the older ones married and stayed in either Somerset or Cambria Country.

13. **Moses Kauffman**, born 1804; died 1872; married Lydia Plank, born 1806; died 1886. She was the sister of Rebecca, wife of his brother Jacob. They moved to Holmes County, Ohio, where he is listed in the census of 1830 along with his brother Jacob, in Salt Creek township. In the 1850 census of Middlebury Township, Elkhart County, Indiana, Moses and family are listed. Moses' age is listed as forty-four and Lydia's as forty-eight, which differs slightly from *AAMG*. Showing that the census is not always accurate, Kauffman is spelled "Coughman"! Moses must have had a cold at the time! He is said to have been a minister in the Amish Church, according to *AAMG*, under Jacob and Catherine's children, but the symbol is missing under Moses and Lydia's family. [101] They had six sons and six daughters.

This ends the chronicle of the family of Catherine Miller and Jacob Kauffman. It is probably the largest of the families of the children of John Miller, Sr. Yet it is typical in that some of the descendants stayed in Pennsylvania, while others moved west with the frontier. Some kept their Amish faith and belong to the Old Order Amish to this day. Others evolved into groups that assimilated more with the outside world, such as the Mennonites and Brethren. Still others joined other churches and went into occupations besides farming, the usual work in the older times. The will and estate settlement that Jacob Kauffman left gives us an unusual insight into what items were used on the farm, and how the heirs divided the goods and money left behind. It is rather touching that Jacob wished to keep the inheritance for his son Christian, in case they again had contact with him. [102]

---

[101] Most of the information on this page is from the will of Jacob Kauffman, 1825, in the Somerset Co. Courthouse. Also, *AAMG*.

[102] *Ibid.*

VI. The Family of "Glades" Christian Miller and Freny (?Blough)

Christian Miller, sixth child of John Miller, Sr., and his wife Magdalena (?Lehman), was born ca1760 in Berks County, Pennsylvania. He traveled with his parents to Somerset County ca1775 and settled with them on the first farm they lived on in Elklick Township. Along with the younger children, he must have helped to clear the land for farming in order to be able to subsist in the wilderness. He had three older brothers, who were all married after the first few years in Somerset. The father, John, had an earlier warrant in the Glades area of Brothers Valley Township, but he chose to live at first on the land which he had purchased in Elklick Township. John's brother Nicholas also had a warrant in Brothers Valley next to his, but he never came to claim it. Perhaps it was for this reason that John chose to stay in Elklick with his younger children, since former neighbors such as the Hochstetlers were living nearby. There were other settlers living in the Glades, such as the family of Benedict Lehman, John, Sr.'s fellow passenger on the ship to America, and others. At any rate, John and Nicholas held on to their land. It appears that Christian's older brother, Jacob, did live there for a few years. It was later that Christian's name was linked to the Glades.

In 1785 Christian would have been twenty-five years old. My interpretation of the sequence of events is that John, Sr., and the younger children stayed on the Elklick property while his older son Jacob, and perhaps others were beginning to clear the land in Brothers Valley. No doubt as Christian became older he also worked with his brothers in the Glades. He was then married to a wife named Freny, not yet identified in any document. If Christian was in the Glades for a while, he must have been acquainted with the young people in the Amish community. One neighbor, Christian Blough, had a sister Freny who has been linked to no other person. That is a strong clue that this was the Freny that Christian married. [103] Other reasons came later, after Christian had lived and worked in the Glades for a number of years. He, like the Bloughs, followed the northern movement toward the Quemahoning region, where Christian eventually settled near the Bloughs.

---

[103] *AAMG*, p. 27.

The year 1785 was a crucial one for the Millers. They had been farming the Elklick property for ten years. John, Jr., Jacob, and Peter were looking for more permanent homesteads of their own. Barbara was married and living near Meyersdale. As it turned out, the three older brothers all found farms in Elklick or Summit Townships. The father had an offer to sell his Elklick farm to Peter Livengood, whose oldest son was recently married.[104] Christian was the oldest son not yet settled, and perhaps already working on the Glades property. The father decided to sell and move to the Glades. The warrant had not been properly surveyed, so a new survey and a new (perhaps the first) proper warrant was issued first to the father, and then in the name of Christian.[105] Thus, Christian had a stake in the Glades property.

The area is called the Glades because it is in a valley north of Berlin, with the stream Stony Creek running through it, enough to give it a good water supply. The Glades area also included the southern area of Stony Creek Township, where members of the Yoder family had extensive farms. The farm was put in Christian's name, but after the Elklick Township farm was sold, the whole family moved to Brothers Valley. My guess is that Christian and his younger brother, Joseph, had been there before the deed was made over to Christian. Joseph had recently been married to Barbara, the daughter of a neighbor, Christian Speicher. By 1786, the Glades tract became a kind of Miller enclave, with Christian and Joseph and their wives, John Miller, Sr., his wife, and four younger daughters.

It was Christian Yoder of Stony Creek Township and Christian Blough of Brothers Valley who first began to promote migration to the Quemahoning region. It was a large area, then called Quemahoning Township, that included present day Stony Creek, Quemahoning, Jenner, and Conemaugh Townships. It was the general pattern for an area not yet settled. Lower Somerset County was settled first because it had more access to roads. These families soon heard about land that had not yet been settled. One wonders why they would want to go further if their present land was not completely cleared. It was the feeling of the times, and the Miller brothers, Christian and Joseph, were also affected. Some of the Bloughs were already there.

When John Miller, Sr., died in 1798, Christian was already investigating land possibilities. There is a warrant for Christian Miller in Quemahoning Township dated 1810, on Bens Creek, which could place it anywhere from the northern limits of Somerset County in Conemaugh Township to the source of Bens Creek in Jenner Township to the southwest. In the 1820 census records can be found the names of Christian Miller and sons Jacob and Solomon. The farms have not been positively identified, but according to *AAMG* and other traditions, that is where Glades Christian settled after leaving the Glades ca1810. Here the question is answered as to why Christian is called Glades Christian: not because he was living in the Glades, but because he came from the Glades, and to identify him in an area where there were several Christian Millers. The tract in Jenner Township that could be that of Glades Christian was issued in 1810, when Jenner

---

[104] Lois Ann Mast, *The Peter Leibundgutt Journal* (Elverson, Pa.: 1991), p. 1.
[105] Land records, Plat Book, 1785, Somerset Co. Courthouse.

was still part of Quemahoning Township. It is next to Peter Blough, who was the nephew of Christian's wife Freny, if we accept that she was a Blough. It was near the western border of Conemaugh Township. Other neighbors were George Smiley and Peter Dellenbach.[106]

This is not the end of the moves of Glades Christian Miller. In the 1830 census, he is listed in Conemaugh Township as Glades Christian, to distinguish him from Schmidt Christian Miller and Keim Christian Miller. He is listed in the census as age eighty,[107] which would make him born in 1750. At any rate, he is called Glades Christian, whether the age is right or not.

There is one other relevant deed concerning one of the Christian Millers. The confusing thing is that Christian Glades and Christian Schmidt both lived in the Jerome area near the present day Blough Mennonite Church. There is a tract of land on the White Thorn Run not far from Jerome, dated 1827, having 100 acres, reserved for a tanyard by the land of George Bierden and Martin Riley. It was signed by John Miller and Joseph Miller, and by Christian Miller and the mark of his wife, Freny. We know that Schmidt Miller had a farm nearer to Jerome, and is buried there. *AAMG* assumes that the tract signed by Christian Miller and wife Freny is for Christian Schmidt Miller and his second wife, Freny. But where is the proof that he had a second wife Freny?[108] He had no sons Joseph and John. I am inclined to think that this either was the retirement home of Glades Christian Miller and his wife Freny, or that he was buying it for his sons John and Joseph to use as a tanyard, as the deed states.[109]

Fortunately we have the will of Glades Christian Miller dated 1840, in which all his heirs are named.[110] At that time he was living in Conemaugh Township. In the census of 1850 the following were living in Conemaugh Township who were children of this family: Peter Miller, age fifty-three, and his wife Mary, age forty-five; Catherine, age sixty-three and her husband, Christian Gindlesberger; Solomon Miller, age fifty, and his wife Anna, age forty-three, and Jacob Thomas, age fifty, widower of daughter Freny, with his second wife, Rachel Miltenberger,[111] age thirty-four. The executors of his will were his son Solomon and Daniel Eash.

The presence of Daniel Eash perhaps gives a clue to Christian Miller's last place of residence. If he was at the White Thorn Run farm, he would have been about a mile or two from the area where the Eash family lived. Peter Miller's farm was also in the area, if one follows the census taker. The approximate location was the road between Jerome and Davidsville. Solomon's home was farther north in the vicinity of the Stahl Mennonite Church and the so-called Soap Hollow, near Johnstown Mennonite School.

Glades Christian Miller died in 1838, if the marker in the oldest part of the cemetery of the Thomas Mennonite Cemetery is his. It replaced an earlier

---

[106] Plat Book, Somerset Co. Courthouse.
[107] 1830 Census, Conemaugh Twp.
[108] Deed Book, Somerset Co. Courthouse.
[109] *Ibid.*
[110] Will, Somerset Co. Courthouse.
[111] *Ibid.*

stone that said simply "CM 1838." Beside him was his wife Freny, "FM." In the same cemetery are the stones of his daughter Freny, married to Jacob Thomas, and Jacob's second wife, Rachel. [112] The Thomas church was not built until about 1870, but local people verify that the lower part (south) was used as an Amish graveyard years before that. Almost all the members of the Thomas Mennonite Church are of Amish ancestry. [113]

At his death, Glades Christian may have had only his younger children living with him in Conemaugh Township: Solomon, Peter, Barbara, and Catherine, all married, and Anna, who was single. Freny, married to Jacob Thomas, had died; Jacob had gone to Iowa; Joseph and John probably went to Ohio after the transaction with the property involving the tanyard at White Thorn Run, which concerned those two sons. It may be that the father was buying it for a business for them, and they possibly did run a tanyard in the 1830s. We don't know when Freny, the mother, died, but possibly the parents were staying near the home of Jacob Thomas, and that is the reason for being buried in the Thomas Cemetery.

Old gravestones at Thomas Mennonite Church near Thomas Mills, Conemaugh Township, Somerset County, Pennsylvania, showing Christian Miller, who died in 1838 (Glades Christian). Also probably his wife, Freny, and his daughter Freny and her husband, Jacob Thomas, and Jacob's second wife, Rachel (Miltenberger). Others of the Kauffman family are buried here of Glades Christian's sister Catherine's family. (Not the parents.)

---

[112] Plat Book, Somerset Co. Courthouse.
[113] *History of Thomas Mennonite Church.*

A Miller farm across the line in Jenner Township from Thomas Mills. Could it be Glades Christian's homestead?

The Children of "Glades" Christian Miller and Freny (?Blough)

1. **John Miller** was the first heir listed in the estate settlement. *AAMG* calls him "a son-in-law, or less likely, a son." But there was a Hannes Miller, as yet unidentified, from near Canton, Ohio, who attended an Amish ministers' meeting in nearby Wayne County, which Jacob Miller of Tuscarawas County, brother of Glades Christian, and Moses Bitschi of Holmes County, Ohio, married to the daughter of John Miller, Jr., thus the niece of Glades Christian, also attended.[114] If this Hannes was the oldest son of Glades Christian, he was meeting with his uncle and the husband of his cousin. This Hannes had a brother who also appeared in the vicinity of Canton. There was a small Amish settlement near Canton in the early nineteenth century.

    From the above information, I conclude that this is the "lost" John Miller. The ministers' conference took place when Glades Christian was still living. The reference with the names of sons John and Joseph about the tract of 100 acres, with part of it reserved for a tanyard, concerns the father and the same two sons. The date was 1827 and could have preceded a move to Ohio. The 100 acres could have included a retirement home for the parents and perhaps a business for the two brothers. It evidently did not work out that way, but the parents may have continued to live there.

---

[114] *Mennonite Quarterly Review,* Amish Ministers' Conference, 1826-31.

There was other evidence of a minister named John Miller who served the church near Canton. He may have been chosen in the lot as was the custom, shortly after he came to Ohio; or, he could have been chosen minister in Pennsylvania. A John Miller can be located on a farm in Canton Township, near other farmers with names such as Yoder, Gerber, Wengerd, and Snavely. There is an estate settlement that seems to refer to this Hannes Miller: [115]

Translation from German (summary): John Miller, Twp. #10, range 8, NW 1/4 section, wife Anna, 1852. Witnesses: George Yutzy, Johannes Jaggi.

There are no children mentioned, but there is one that could fit in *DBH* #3086, in which Emanuel Yoder of Canton is married to Elizabeth Miller. Since there are no other children mentioned, it must be left to future research to see if there are others, and indeed, to verify this hypothesis: 1. Barbara, born ca1812; married William (?Gerber). 2. Elizabeth, born 1818; married Emanuel Yoder, and moved to Smithville, Ohio. There may be others.

2. **Jacob J. Miller**, born 1784 in Somerset County, Pennsylvania; died 1853; married Catherine Lewis, born in Ireland. They moved to Guthrie County, Iowa. [116]
3. **Mary Miller**, born 1782 in Somerset County; died 1853; married Isaac Kauffman, born 1776; died 1862. They lived in Juniata County, Pennsylvania. They had fourteen children, two of which died young. Seven sons and five daughters had families.
4. **Barbara Miller**, born ca1784; married John Menges. They lived in Jenner Township, Somerset County.
5. **Catherine Miller**, born ca1787 in Somerset County; married Christian Gindelsberger, born ca1787. They lived in Conemaugh Township, Somerset County. They had four sons and seven daughters.
6. **Christian Glades Miller**, born in Somerset County; married Esther Lewis, born in Ireland. In 1820 they were living in Jenner Township, Somerset County; moved to Greencastle Township, Putnam County, Indiana. They had three sons and three daughters.
7. **Joseph Miller**, born ca1793 in Somerset County; married Elizabeth ___ as his first wife and had three children. One son married Magdalena Gindelsberger and lived in Smithville, Ohio; they had four sons and two daughters. They were not Mennonite. Son Jacob and wife are buried in Smithville Cemetery. [117]
8. **Anna Miller**, born in Somerset County ca1794; single. Probably lived with her parents and cared for them in their old age. She bought many things at the sale of her parents' possessions. She died in Conemaugh Township.
9. **Peter G. Miller**, born ca1796; died 1807; married Mary Kimmel. Their home must have been in the area between Jerome and Davidsville. Two of their sons, Isaac and Henry, are buried in the Blough Mennonite Cemetery, east of Jerome. Peter and Mary had five sons: Abraham, Isaac, David, Peter, and Henry.

---

[115] Wills, Stark Co. Courthouse, Canton, Ohio.
[116] The following names are given as in *AAMG*, except for #1, in which John is a son.
[117] Wayne Co., Ohio, cemetery records, Wooster, Ohio, Library.

10. **Solomon Miller**, born in Somerset County, Pennsylvania, in 1797. The name of his first wife is not known. They had one daughter, Magdalena, who married John Sala, a well-known furniture maker and craftsman.[118] They lived in the region of Soap Hollow and the Stahl Mennonite Church. Solomon married Anna Thomas after the death of his first wife. They had one son and seven daughters.
11. **Freny Miller**, born ca1798; died by 1840; married Jacob Thomas, born ca1798; died by 1880. He married 2) Rachel Miltenberger, born 1816. In the 1850 Census they were living in Conemaugh Township. They are buried in the Amish cemetery of the Thomas Mennonite Church in the oldest section. Freny and Jacob had three children: Anna, Peter, and Catherine.

---

[118] Booklet on the work of John Sala.

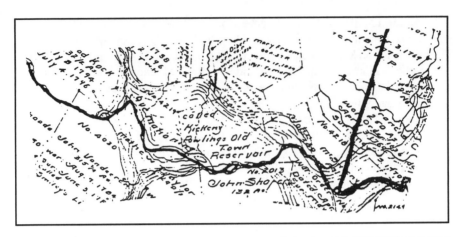

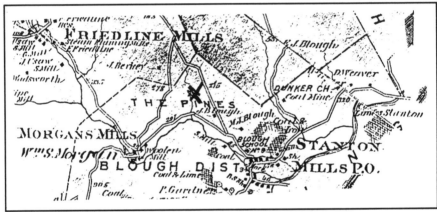

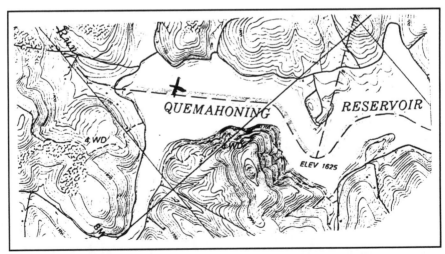

The Joseph Miller farm at three periods: a. Plat map of Jenner Township showing the Joseph Miller farm; b. Atlas of 1875; and c. Present-day map showing the dam.

VII. The Family of Joseph Miller and
1) Barbara Speicher and
2) Barbara Bontrager

Joseph Miller, the fifth son of John Miller, Sr., was, like the others, born in Berks County. His birth date is not known exactly, but it was perhaps two years after Christian, his next older brother, ca1762. Christian and Joseph are sometimes associated, because they lived in some of the same areas. After coming with his parents to Somerset County, he lived with his parents and family in Elklick Township, and as the others did, spent some time in the Glades.

When the older children moved to farms of their own, it was Christian and Joseph who began to develop the tract in Brothers Valley. It must have been then that Joseph became acquainted with Barbara Speicher, the daughter of neighbor Christian Speicher. They had both come with their families from Berks County, and probably knew each other from childhood. The Speichers, however, lived in Cumru Township in Berks County, which was some distance south, near Reading.[119] Christian Speicher, Sr., was with the early delegation to Somerset County to look for land that first brought Joseph's father, John, Sr., so it was natural for Joseph to marry Barbara and have the other Speichers next door.

The situation changed when all the remaining Millers came to the Glades. John, Sr., the father, had the land but wished to have his next oldest son associated with it. We don't know what arrangement was made, but the Speicher lands were considerably larger than that of John, Sr. It could be that Joseph and Barbara farmed or cleared a portion of the Speicher property during their marriage. At the same time, Christian Miller and his brother Joseph were said to be involved in operating the Miller farm. This part is unclear, but there is probably some truth in both—that the two brothers worked together, and that Joseph and his wife Barbara were also helping the Speichers. The truth is that Joseph, like Christian, had no intention of staying in the Glades, and soon after the death of their father, they were looking northward to new lands. Shortly after 1800 when both of the elder Millers and Speichers had died, at least the fathers, Joseph himself became a widower. His wife Barbara died after bearing six children.

---

[119] Tax records, Cumru Twp., Berks Co., Pa.

The Children of Joseph Miller and Barbara Speicher [120]

1. **(Anna) Miller**, born ca1783, married Henry (?Miller), son of Christian Miller (Keim Christian Miller), according to *AAMG*; the name of this daughter is uncertain because only Henry is mentioned in the estate settlement. They lived in Conemaugh Township, Somerset County, Pennsylvania, and had six sons and three daughters. One of their daughters, Rebecca, was married to Nathan Smiley, an Irish orphan who was raised in an Amish-Mennonite home in Conemaugh Township. Nathan and Rebecca moved to Elkhart County, Indiana. Nathan's son from a previous marriage was John Smiley who was a Mennonite preacher in Indiana and Ohio.
2. **Jost Miller** was born about 1786 and married a wife named Mary. They lived in Conemaugh Township, Somerset County. Not much is known about him, but according to *AAMG*, they had seven children, four sons and three daughters, all with question marks, indicating that we are not sure about even the children's names. The children, at least, do not seem to be either Amish or Mennonite.
3. **Elizabeth Miller**, born 1789, died 1852, married Henry Blough, son of Jacob Blough, oldest son of Christian Blough of Lebanon County, an immigrant of 1750. Henry's older brother was Jacob Blough, one of the earliest ministers of the Amish in Conemaugh Township. Henry and Elizabeth were living in Jenner Township in 1820 near her father Joseph Miller. They were probably members of the Amish church in the southern part of Conemaugh Township near Jerome where Christian "Schmidt" Miller was the bishop. In 1850, Henry and Elizabeth were living in Conemaugh Township near their nephew Henry, son of his brother Jacob. Henry and Elizabeth had only two daughters, Anna married to Jonathan Eash, and Freny married to Jonas Weaver. In the 1850 census, Henry Blough, age sixty-seven, and Elizabeth, age sixty-one, had living with them Henry Eash, their grandson, age eighteen, and Jacob Blough, age ten, son of Jacob Blough, a minister, and son of Henry's brother Jacob, the early minister. The son was also a minister or deacon.
4. **A daughter**, not named, according to *AAMG*, possibly married to a John Miller. They suggest John Miller, the son of Broad Run John Miller, but there are many question marks in their book, and in my mind as well.
5. **Magdalena Miller**, born ca1796, married Stephen Kauffman. They moved to Holmes County, Ohio, where they were living in 1830 in German Township. They had ten children, seven of whom raised families. Stephen died in Holmes County, but Magdalena then moved with her son, Benjamin, and family to Elkhart County, Indiana, where she died in 1857.
6. **Mary Miller**, born about 1800, married Joseph Hostetler. They moved to La Porte County, Indiana. They had three sons and three daughters belonging to different churches with the majority in the Church of the Brethren.

---

[120] Information from *AAMG*, and *Mennonite Encyclopedia*.

John Bontrager was a more recent immigrant, having come to America with his father, Martin, in 1767, shortly before the move to Somerset County. He came to Elklick Township with his two brothers, Andrew and Christian, where each briefly held land before moving on. [121] He may have also passed through the Glades before taking up land in Quemahoning Township, just north of the Quemahoning River, where he was living in 1810. [122] It was about that time, or a little before, that Joseph married another Barbara, who was the daughter of John Bontrager. This gave Joseph the chance to leave the Glades and move north. In 1815 Joseph was issued a plot in Jenner Township on Quemahoning Creek from Samuel Berkey, on land adjoining William McSummy and John Bontrager. [123] This was at the extreme south of Jenner Township, and so close to Conemaugh Township that part of the property was across the line. Joseph may have added to his original land, because in 1835 when he deeded his land to his son Joseph, Jr., he was paid $2,000 rather than the $200 he had paid twenty years before. [124]

Joseph and his second wife had five more children who grew up on the farm in Jenner Township. In 1835 he transferred the property to his son Joseph, who operated it until he moved to Indiana some time before 1850. By that time Joseph, Sr.'s children from his first marriage were married and settled in other places in Pennsylvania. His daughter Elizabeth was married to Henry Blough and lived in Jenner Township, not far from Joseph's homestead, but a bit further north nearer the border of Conemaugh Township. [125] All five of Joseph's children from Barbara Bontrager moved to Lagrange County, Indiana. [126] It is not known exactly when Joseph and Barbara died, but it must have been some years before 1850, after which his children left for Indiana.

Joseph's homestead was not far from Stanton Mills, a small town on the Quemahoning River. Shortly after 1900, a dam was built over the Quemahoning River, which completely inundated the town of New Stanton, a small Brethren church that was in the vicinity, and the homestead farm of Joseph and his wife Barbara. Their graves are undoubtedly also at the bottom of the reservoir formed by the dam.

The Children of Joseph Miller and Barbara Bontrager [127]

1. **Sarah Miller**, born 1803, Jenner Township, Somerset County, Pennsylvania; married to Philip Weirich. They moved to Lagrange County, Indiana. They had five sons and one daughter; Amish-Mennonite.
2. **Daniel S. Miller**, born 1806; died 1886; married 1) Barbara Hostetler, born 1810; died 1861. They moved to Lagrange County, Indiana. They had two

---

[121] Tax records, Elklick Twp., Somerset Co., Pa.
[122] *Ibid.*, 1810.
[123] Plat map of Jenner Twp.
[124] Deed, Somerset Co. Courthouse.
[125] 1820 census, Jenner Twp.
[126] Census records, Lagrange Co., Ind. *AAMG*.
[127] *AAMG*. Census records.

sons and four daughters; Amish-Mennonite. He married 2) Barbara Eash, born 1807; died 1891.
3. **Joseph J. Miller**, born 1808, Somerset County, Pennsylvania; married to Elizabeth Yoder, born 1812/14; died 1881. They moved to Lagrange County, Indiana, where he was a bishop in the Amish-Mennonite Church. They had two sons and three daughters.
4. **John S. Miller**, born 1811; died 1861; married Margaret Sutter, born ca1815. They moved to Lagrange County, Indiana. They had three sons, and a daughter who died at age eight; Amish-Mennonite.
5. **Freny Miller**, born 1815; died 1887; married Joseph Hershberger, born 1811; died 1891. They moved from Somerset County to Lagrange County, Indiana. They had two sons and seven daughters. They belonged to the Amish-Mennonite Church.

"In the following year of 1841, four families made preparations to move to Indiana: Daniel S. and Barbara Miller and five children (Samuel, Polly, Jonathan, Rachel, and Barbara), Pre. Joseph and Elizabeth Miller and four children (Lydia, Polly, Daniel, and Joseph), Deacon Joseph and Barbara Borntreger and five children (Elizabeth, Christian, Barbara, Hansi [John E.*] and David), and Christian and Elizabeth Borntrager and two children (Lydia and Maria). These four families loaded their most necessary things on wagons, of which each family had one, and three one-horse spring wagons, for at that time there were no railroads. (*Author of this history)[128]

Accounts of the first Amish-Mennonite settlers in Elkhart, and then Lagrange County, Indiana, in 1841. Two of the men were sons of Joseph Miller, and the other two families were their cousins, the sons of John Bontrager, Jr., the brother of Barbara, the wife of Joseph Miller, Sr.

"On June 3, 1841, these twenty-four persons left Somerset County, Pennsylvania, and set out westward. First we drove by way of Holmes County, Ohio, where we visited one week, then went on toward Indiana. We came through the State of Michigan, through White Pigeon, then southwestwardly to the Indiana line, where we had our last camp night. The next day we drove through Middlebury and reached Goshen, Elkhart County, Indiana, on June 29. Then we drove three miles further southward on the west side of the Elkhart Prairie and lived there several months in small cabins.

"But the nice prairie-land was then already too expensive for them, since they had little money; therefore they looked around for timber land. Joseph Miller and Joseph Bontrager each bought 80 acres in Clinton Township; Daniel S. Miller and Christian Bontrager went ten miles northeastward to Newbury Township, Lagrange County, and bought homesteads there. And so each moved onto his land."[129]

---

[128] John E. Bontrager, *History of the Amish-Mennonites in Indiana* (1907).
[129] *Ibid.*

VIII. The Family of Maria Miller and John Schrock, Jr.

John Miller, Sr., had five daughters in all, mostly younger than his sons. With the exception of Catherine Kauffman, the other four all moved with their parents to their farm in the Glades ca1786. If we assume that Maria was the oldest of these younger daughters and was born ca1764, she would have been twenty-two years of age, just the age of marriageability, although many were married at a much younger age. Probably Maria was no stranger to the Glades, especially if we assume that John the father already had the warrant back in 1771. Jacob, Maria's older brother, was probably there for several years, and now brother Christian was a kind of co-owner with her father.

Nicholas Miller, her father's uncle, had a farm next to theirs that was not properly owned and cultivated, as Nicholas, after taking out the warrant, did not come to Bedford County at all. In fact, he had died in Berks County in 1784. We must remember that even in 1785, this land was not yet cleared. A small area to raise a bit of grain and vegetables, a cow or two, and a cabin to live in was all that a pioneer of those days could expect. John the father needed a much larger house if it was to hold the entire family, which consisted of John, Sr., and his wife Magdalena, Christian and his wife and perhaps two children, Joseph and his wife and perhaps one child, and the four unmarried daughters. The farm perhaps resembled a series of cabins to accommodate these people. Joseph had connections with the Speichers next door, and Christian with the Bloughs, and the whole Amish community was ready to help wherever possible, as they had a long tradition of mutual aid.

Maria in that case would have been familiar with the community and had already made friends. The Schrags or Schrocks, as the Americans called them, were fairly recent immigrants from Europe. Johannes Schrag, with his second wife and older son Johannes, or John in English, came from Europe in 1766, only twenty years before.[130] His younger brother Casper also came along. John, Jr., was almost as old as Casper and so one can imagine them operating as a family unit, to set down roots. First a warrant was issued in the Glades in 1774

---

[130] Strassburger and Hinke, land and tax records.

in Casper's name. No doubt they all helped to clear the land at first. Casper was already married to Maria Stuckey, whom he perhaps learned to know back in Lebanon County, where they had spent their first years after immigration.

By the time the Millers arrived, John Schrock, Sr., had remarried and had several children by his second wife, Elizabeth. In fact, his first three children were girls, but the next, Christian, was a boy. In 1786 a warrant was taken in Christian's name for 172+ acres in Elklick, now Summit Township, south of the Casselman River. Like John Miller, Sr., he moved with his younger children to the new farm, leaving the Glades property to Casper, with John, Jr., to help him.

We do not know at what point John Schrock, Jr., was married to Maria Miller, but it must have been shortly before or shortly after these events. It is difficult to say where each of these families lived. Maria must have been at least ten years younger than John Schrock, Jr. Both Casper and John, Jr., had large families, so it was not practical to farm the same place together after the children were old enough to help. In addition, Casper's older brother Ulrich came to America later, in 1769. After perhaps spending a few years on farms in and around Reading in Berks County, he moved to Somerset County, probably spending some time with his wife's brother, Hans Christner, in Elklick Township before settling in the Glades. Uli, as he was called, had an older son John, born in 1776, to add to the confusion of keeping all the John Schrocks straight. Casper also called his second son John, born in 1778.

About all we can say is that Maria and John must have had a house and some acreage on one of the pioneer farms, since there doesn't seem to be a deed issued to them. They had nine children, so they needed some land to live on and produce food. Their home was probably on Casper's warrant, as that appears to be Schrock family land. John Schrock does appear on a tax list for Brothers Valley in 1796, so he must have had some land.

John Schrock, Jr., died at a relatively early age in 1813, having been born ca1754. He would have been fifty-nine, but Maria was ten years younger. John's grave is a single marker in a farm cemetery on the original homestead of Christian Speicher. Thomas Maust II, in his study of the Glades Amish homesteads, states that "John Schrock purchased land from the Speichers."[131] When John died, a note from the Orphans Court, quoted by *AAMG*, states that "the widow Mary renounces the right to administer the estate to Daniel Miller and Michael Troyer." These were Daniel, her nephew, son of John, Jr., and his father-in-law, Michael Troyer, Jr. She was left with nine children, the oldest of whom was thirty and the youngest was only six. Four were under twenty.

---

[131] Thomas Maust II, *The Amish in Brothers Valley Township*, in Berlin, Pa., Centennial Book (see Appendix No. 2).

The Children of Maria Miller and John Schrock, Jr. [132]

1. **John Schrock**, born 1783; date of death unknown; married, but his wife's name is unknown. According to *AAMG*, they lived in the town of Berlin, county seat of Brothers Valley Township, Somerset County. Their children, according to a baptismal record, were: Dorothea, Elizabeth, John, Michael, Caroline, Frantz, James J., and Susanna. Place of residence, unknown. Four sons and four daughters.
2. **Joseph Schrock**, born 1784; died 1870; lived in Summit Township, Somerset County, Pennsylvania. In the 1850 census, Summit Township, were Joseph Schrock, age sixty-six; wife Rosanne, age fifty-two; and one child, Mary, age twenty-seven. According to *AAMG*, there were four children: Samuel, Elizabeth, Mary, and Jacob.
3. **Gertrude Schrock**, born 1786; died 1836; married Joseph J. Yoder, born 1788; died 1863. They lived in Elklick Township until 1836, the year of Gertrude's death. He then married Juliana Ramsberger and lived at Davidsville in Conemaugh Township. Gertrude and Joseph had three children: Benjamin, Veronica, and Elizabeth. He had nine children in his second marriage.
4. **Barbara Schrock**, born 1788; death date unknown; married John Klingaman, born ca1779. They lived in Elklick Township, Somerset County, Pennsylvania. Number in family unknown; Church of the Brethren.
5. **Jacob Schrock**, born 1790; died 1856; married Barbara Fike, born 1786; died 1861. They lived in Milford Township, Somerset County. They had three sons: Daniel, Joseph, and Christian; Church of the Brethren.
6. **Magdalena Schrock**, born 1793; death date unknown; Summit Township, Somerset County, Pennsylvania; Church of the Brethren.
7. **Fanny Schrock**, born 1795; death date unknown; married John Blough, born 1794; died 1866. They lived in Quemahoning Township, Somerset County. They had four sons and four daughters that raised families, and several that died young; Church of the Brethren.
8. **Yost Schrock**, born 1798; death date unknown; married Margaret, family name unknown. They lived in Elklick Township in 1830. They had twelve children; of them seven daughters and four sons grew to maturity. The last four were born in Garret County, Maryland, indicating that the parents moved there.
9. **Aaron Schrock**, born 1805; death date unknown; married Catherine Meyers, born 1805; died 1840. They lived in Upper Turkeyfoot Township, Somerset County. They had four children, two sons and two daughters.

The family of John Schrock and Maria Miller differs a bit from the others, because most of them stayed in Somerset County. On the other hand, they lived in parts of Somerset County that the others did not, who seemed to have had

---

[132] *AAMG*.

close family ties. Yet Maria and John Schrock both came from the same Amish-Mennonite background. Several of the children's families joined the German Baptist Brethren, or Church of the Brethren, which was normal for those who did not move west. In Ohio, Indiana, and Iowa they were much more likely to join other Amish-Mennonites who were forming settlements in the west. One family, that of Yost Schrock, stayed in Somerset County for a while and they moved to Garret County, Maryland, where many families from Somerset County re-formed and made new Amish-Mennonite communities.[133]

---

[133] Study of *AAMG* and census lists of Pa. and Md.

IX. The Family of Freny Miller and Christian Speicher, Jr.

The paths of the Millers and the Speichers have crossed and come together numerous times. Ulrich Speicher came on the *Charming Nancy* with the earliest Millers in 1737. Their warrants in Bern Township in Berks County were near each other. Christian Speicher, Sr., and John Miller, Sr., were together in the first group to obtain warrants to settle in Somerset County in 1771. Their warrants were side-by-side in the Glades, although John Miller did not come to claim his until 1786. However, as pointed out before, there were numerous opportunities to get together. They attended the same church; the Millers came frequently to inspect their claim in the Glades; and the young people got together frequently.

Joseph Miller was the first to cement relations with the Speichers when he and Barbara Speicher were married. Joseph and Christian Miller more or less took over the farm in the Glades. The Speichers and the Millers were on one side of the Stony Creek, which gave them a good water supply, and Nicholas Miller's land was on the other side, for the time being unoccupied. Christian Speicher had been living in Cumru Township, near Reading in Berks County, Pennsylvania, before coming across the mountains. It is not known whether he took his family along this first time, but it is doubtful, since most of the others returned to get their possessions and families a few years later, after they had wound up their affairs at home.[134]

Christian Speicher, Sr.'s, family consisted of his wife and sons Samuel, Christian, John, and Joseph, and daughters Anna and Barbara. Anna later married John Stutzman, and Barbara married Joseph Miller. To cement the connection even further, sons Joseph and Christian, Jr., married two of John, Sr.,'s daughters. They would have been barely twenty when John Miller and his whole family came in 1786, but within a few years three Millers were married to Speichers. Part of Christian Speicher's land was across the line in Stony Creek Township, but it was really only one tract of 325+ acres, enough land to keep all the extended family busy.[135] They also had some additional acreage in Stony Creek

---

[134] From *AAMG*. Tax records. Warrant lists.
[135] Plat map of Brothers Valley Twp.

Township not adjacent to their other land. Christian Speicher, Sr., owned the land until his death ca1797, when his will was probated, now filed at the courthouse in Somerset. His widow was Christina, sister of Joseph Mishler, also of the Glades.

This history is about the Miller family, but as shown by this discussion, all the Amish-Mennonite families in a given community are closely interrelated. We will first consider Christian Speicher, Jr., who was married to Freny Miller sometime between her birth ca1766 and the birth of their first child ca1786. Therefore, they were probably married just before or just after the Millers came to the Glades permanently. Christian, Jr., and his bride doubtless had a cabin and a piece of the family property set off for them. In the 1790 census there are a number of Speichers mentioned as family heads, one after another: Christian, Sr., and Jr., Samuel, John, and Joseph, presumably all with families on the same tract. With Joseph Miller and John Stutzman married to the daughters, they had a virtual army for the 325 acres. In 1820, Christian and John Spiker (as it is anglicized) are in Brothers Valley Township, while Joseph, Sr., and Jr., are in Stony Creek. [136]

There is another factor in the story. Back in Lebanon County where many of the Amish families lived for a while, there were other churches that had a strong influence on the Amish. One of their ministers, Abraham Drachsel, joined a group called the United Brethren who, like the Methodists, had a strong missionary message asking people to repent of their sins. The difference between the Methodists and the United Brethren was that the latter had revival meetings in German, which drew great crowds of the German-speaking settlers.

The Gnaegi family, who had moved from Berks County to Lebanon, were especially influenced. Christian Gnaegi had settled near Meyersdale, but his daughter Magdalena, married to Jacob Blough, was living near Berlin. Christian Newcomer, a former Mennonite, wrote a journal telling of his years as a circuit rider preacher, and one of his usual stops was at Berlin to stay with Jacob Blough. There were very few who had joined them in the Berlin area, but the circuit rider system allowed evangelists to preach in houses in communities where there were only a few converts. [137] They had some competition with the German Baptists, or Dunkards, who were especially strong in Stony Creek Township.

Some of the Amish were reluctant to join the Dunkards because of the requirement to be rebaptized by immersion. The United Brethren did not require this, only that they be converted and live a good life. A number of the Glades Amish went to hear Reverend Newcomer when he preached at Jacob Blough's home in Berlin. I have no documentary evidence, but I suspect that Christian Speicher and his wife sometimes attended their services. Some of the other Bloughs had already joined the Dunkards and Christian Gnaegi was preparing to move to Scio, Ohio, where there was a United Brethren community rather than an Amish group. He eventually became a preacher in that church, even though his son Johannes stayed with the Amish.

---

[136] Study of plat map, census records, and *AAMG*.
[137] Christian Newcomer, *Journal*.

Freny Miller Speicher may have been the only one of John Miller, Sr.'s children to join the United Brethren. She was born ca1766 and was married to her neighbor, Christian Speicher, Jr., ca1788. The Speichers were members of the Amish community, and we presume they were married in the church. The urge to move west was very strong. Perhaps influences like Reverend Newcomer made the urge even stronger as he spoke of churches in Ohio where they lived in larger communities. We do not know whether they moved right away or waited. [138]

In the 1820 census, both Christian and Joseph Speicher were living in Stony Creek Township.[139] Freny's brother Jacob had been an Amish preacher in Somerset County, and now was the first preacher in Tuscarawas County, Ohio. The Dunkards and United Brethren were also settling in Tuscarawas County. We are not sure about the Speicher parents, but by 1840 most of the children and the mother were living in Wayne Township, Wayne County, Ohio. The last record found in the census for both Christian Speicher, Jr., and his wife was in Stony Creek Township in 1820.[140] Presumably Freny Speicher was a widow in 1840, living with one of her children in Wayne Township, Wayne County, Ohio. The family members were all members of the United Brethren Church, and we presume that Freny was, too.

The Children of Freny Miller and Christian Speicher, Jr.

1. **Elizabeth Speicher**, born ca1790; living in Wayne Township, Wayne County, Ohio. Single, perhaps living with her mother.
2. **Abraham Spiker**, born ca1790. His wife's name was Rachel, family name not known. They lived in Wayne Township, Wayne County, Ohio; United Brethren Church. They had two sons and three daughters.
3. **David Spiker**, born 1793; died 1871; married Magdalena Cober, born 1801; died 1887; lived in Wayne Township, Wayne County, Ohio. He was a farmer, and they belonged to the United Brethren Church. They had three sons and one daughter.
4. **Jacob C. Spiker**, born ca1804; died 1880; married 1) Margaret Gindelsberger, born 1811; died 1876. They lived in Wayne County, Ohio; three daughters.
5. **Anna Spiker**, born 1806; death date unknown; married John Shaulis. Other details not known.
6. **Jonathan Spiker**, born 1807; married 1) Catherine Yergin, died 1842; married 2) Elizabeth Weiler (named confirmed by a descendant), born 1810; death date not known. He was a cabinetmaker and lived along the highway between Smithville and Wooster, in Wayne Township, Wayne County, Ohio. He had one son and four daughters from his first marriage, and four daughters and a son in his second marriage. They belonged to the Madisonburg United Brethren Church.[141]

---

[138] Census records. Correspondence with descendants.
[139] Census records.
[140] Study of census records, land records, *AAMG*.
[141] Wayne Co. census and atlas. Correspondence with Mrs. Marjorie Smith, Ashland, Ohio, a descendant.

The graves of David and Jonathan Speicher (Spiker) in the Lutheran Cemetery west of Madisonburg, Wayne County, Ohio. David and Jonathan were the sons of Freny Miller and Christian Speicher, Jr.

X. The Family of (?Susanna) Miller and Christian Mishler

The name of this daughter of John Miller, Sr., is not known for certain, but an examination of names among the descendants leads me to propose the name Susanna. One of Christian Mishler's children and several grandchildren have that name, which is not too common in the Miller family. "Susanna" was born ca1770.[142] She made the same moves as her parents, ending up in the Glades. She would have been about sixteen when they moved to the Brothers Valley farm. Thus, as the young people became acquainted, they began to seek suitable spouses.

Joseph Mishler had moved to the Glades with other pioneers. He had come from Germany with his mother, a brother Jacob, and four sisters in 1749.[143] They came on the ship *Phoenix*, the same ship that Hannes Miller and Benedict Lehman came on. So the Mishler and Miller families were acquainted from Europe. The widow Mishler had the good fortune to marry Christian Zug as his second wife. He was the land agent for numerous warrants in Somerset County, but he stayed at his home in Chester County, where he welcomed many new immigrants. The Mishler children were supported by their stepfather, but eventually they became independent and formed families of their own. They worked on farms near Reading in Cumru Township, where sister Freny was married to Christian Miller (of the family that came in 1742). Her sister Christina was married to Christian Speicher, Sr., who became Hannes Miller's neighbor. We don't know the name of Joseph Mishler's wife, but some think she may have been a Berkey.

Joseph Mishler's farm was in the Glades, a bit west of the Miller and Speicher farms, but still in Brothers Valley. They all attended the Amish church in the Glades. Though their families were frequently in contact, there was no close blood relation.[144]

---

[142] This daughter was born ca1768, according to *AAMG*.
[143] Strassburger and Hinke, ship lists.
[144] Plat map of Brothers Valley Twp., Somerset Co., Pa.

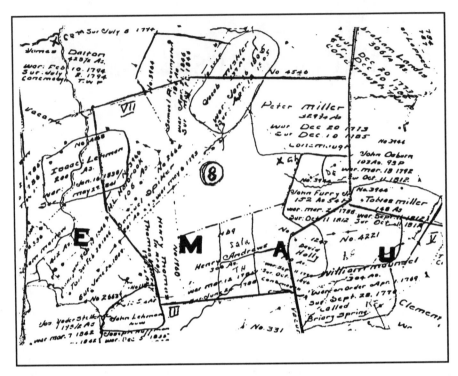

The plat map of the Miller District of Conemaugh Township showing the plat of Jacob Mishler, where nephew Christian Mishler and wife (?Susanna) Miller probably lived.

Christian Mishler was the oldest son of Joseph, born ca1764. Christian and Susanna were married, but instead of beginning farming at home, they followed the example of the Yoders and the Bloughs and moved north to Conemaugh Township. Christian Mishler and his brother-in-law, David Livingston, apparently chose land together, side by side south of Ben's Creek in the northern part of the township, toward Johnstown. It must have been about 1795. There are two early warrants, shown on the Conemaugh Township plat map, one to David Livingston and one to Jacob Mishler, that were only issued in 1805. However, all the Conemaugh plats are later than those in Somerset County.[145] Settlement was later, but not that much.

It appears that the mechanism for registering the warrants was delayed for some reason, but the land was occupied before that. This makes tracing the original plats much more difficult. One of the warrants of 1805 was to Jacob Mishler, who would have been the uncle of Christian Mishler, married to the daughter of Hannes or John Miller, Sr. Jacob Mishler didn't settle here, but his

---

[145] Warrant on plat map, Conemaugh Twp.

application was dated 1805. It was the younger David Livingston and Christian Mishler, the nephew of the Jacob who had been issued the warrant, who lived there.

Apparently the older Livingstons died and Jacob Mishler, who was Brethren according to *AAMG*, moved to communities further west and left the land to his nephew Christian Mishler, who married Susanna. So David and Anna (Mishler) Livingston and Christian and Susanna (Miller) Mishler lived on the two homesteads. It is sometimes difficult to tell which lived on which, although in the first generation at least Livingstons lived on Livingston land and Mishlers lived on Mishler land. In later generations the original tracts broke up (the Mishler land was 337 acres and the Livingston tract was 180 acres). Other Mishlers lived in other areas of Conemaugh Township.[146]

There is an old Mishler Cemetery about five miles north of Thomas Mills which seems to be of the family of Christian's brother Joseph, also a son of Joseph, the pioneer in Brothers Valley. The cemetery contains the graves of Joseph, his son John, and John's son Gabriel, and their wives. It probably does not include the graves of Christian and Susanna.[147] The custom was to have their own farm cemeteries or for perhaps two family farms near each other. They are probably buried on their farm or a neighboring farm.

Another Mishler cemtery which has recently been brought to my attention seems more likely to be on the Christian Mishler homestead. Christian and his wife have no legible markers, but several of their children and grandchildren are buried there. One of the oldest is of Christian Mishler, Jr., in 1858, and his daughter, Susan, and her husband, Isaac Yoder, died 1905, age seventy-nine. Also buried there are Levi Mishler who died in 1897 at age fifty-nine, the son of Tobias Mishler, youngest son of Christian Mishler and (?Susanna) Miller. The cemetery is in the Conemaugh Township, on the farm of Robert Wengerd, and has recently been restored.[148]

The Children of (?Susanna) Miller and Christian Mishler

1. **Barbara Mishler**, born ca1786; married (?David) Livingston; died 1828; lived in Conemaugh Township. They probably lived on a part of the original Livingston-Mishler land. Some question about whether Barbara's name was Mishler, but it seems likely. They had nine known children, seven sons and two daughters.
2. **Infant son**, born ca1788; died before 1800.
3. **Elizabeth Mishler**, born ca1790; died single.

---

[146] Information from plat map.
[147] Cemetery Record Book in State Library, Harrisburg, Pa.
[148] Information from Mr. Rachel Hargreaves, Somerset, Pa.

4. **Peter Mishler**, born 1791; died 1876; married Susanna Berkey, born ca1790. They lived in Mechanic Township, Holmes County, Ohio. They had three sons and three daughters.
5. **Magdalena Mishler**, birth year not known, ca1794; married 1) John Weaver, born ca1786; died 1813. They had one daughter, Susanna. She married 2) David Blough, born 1789; died 1872; as his second wife. They had three daughters; they lived in Conemaugh Township.
6. **Susanna Mishler**, born ca1797; death date unknown; married David Weaver, born 1790; died 1856. They lived in Conemaugh Township, Somerset County, and in Richland Township, Cambria County, Pennsylvania. They had seven sons and four daughters; two of the daughters died single.
7. **Christian Mishler**, born ca1798; died 1859; married Barbara Eash, birth and death dates unknown. They lived in Conemaugh Township. They had ten children, six sons and four daughters.
8. **Catherine Mishler**, born 1800; died 1886. She lived in Conemaugh Township; single.
9. **Jonas Mishler**, born ca1802; died ca1861; married 1) Magdalena(?) Eash. She died and he married 2) Magdalena Thomas, born 1813; died 1898. They lived in Conemaugh Township. They had eleven children, nine of whom raised families; there were seven sons and four daughters, two of whom died young.[149]
10. **Tobias Mishler**, born 1809; died 1878; married Lydia Eash, born 1819; died 1900, as her first husband. They lived in Richland Township, Cambria County, Pennsylvania. They had six sons and two daughters.

Descendants of (?Susanna) Miller and Christian Mishler can now be found in many states, especially in Ohio and Indiana, particularly son Peter's family, who moved first to Ohio. Their son Daniel's family moved on from Ohio to Indiana, Iowa, and Oregon, where Jacob D. Mishler was a minister in the Mennonite Church.[150]

Many descendants stayed in Conemaugh Township or across the county line in Richland Township, Cambria County, near Johnstown. A son of Tobias Mishler is buried at the Stahl Mennonite Cemetery northwest of Davidsville. David Mishler died in 1908 at age sixty-eight.[151] Other descendants moved farther east in the Tire Hill area. They intermarried with others of Hannes Miller's descendants, especially of Catherine Miller and Jacob Kauffman, who also lived in the northern part of Conemaugh Township. The graves and the actual homestead have not yet been found.[152]

---

[149] Most of this material is from *AAMG*.
[150] *Mennonite Encyclopedia*.
[151] Cemetery inscription collected by the author.
[152] Considerable search was done in the area, obviously not enough to be conclusive.

The map on page 78 shows the plats on the original map of Conemaugh Township. It was superimposed on the county atlas map of 1875 to show the school districts, which in this case is Miller District No. 8. It includes the so-called Soap Hollow District, which preceded the present day Johnstown Mennonite School. Nearby was the Stahl Mennonite Church. The Mishlers lived in the northern part of this district. Note the plats of Jacob Mishler and David Livingston. Since these two families intermarried, this homestead of Christian Mishler and the daughter of John Miller, Sr., could be part of either, but the deeds seem to say that Christian finally lived on a part of his uncle Jacob Mishler's plat. It would be north of Soap Hollow and northwest of the Stahl Mennonite Church.

XI. The Family of Elizabeth Miller and Joseph Speicher

*E*lizabeth Miller was married to Joseph Speicher, the brother of her sister's husband, Christian, Jr., and her brother Joseph's first wife, Barbara.[153] They were all children of Christian Speicher, Sr., and grandchildren of Ulrich Speicher, one of the Amish-Mennonite pioneers in the Northkill settlement in Berks County, Pennsylvania. Ulrich was also a shipmate of Jacob Miller on the *Charming Nancy* in 1737, who may have been the father of John Miller, Sr., as discussed earlier.

Their first warrants were near each other in Berks County and their farms were side-by-side in Brothers Valley. Joseph and Elizabeth stayed in Somerset County rather than move west, and they lived in Stony Creek Township rather than stay in Brothers Valley. Joseph had a tract of land next to Isaac Miller, possibly a relative of his wife. Isaac had a warrant dated 1785 for 100 acres; however, another record says that Isaac died in 1785, but that he had lived there since 1777. This might indicate part of the land ownership and occupancy. Isaac lived on the land without a proper warrant of ownership, perhaps with only an application. However, when he died and the heirs wished to sell it, there had to be a warrant. I believe there were hundreds of instances of this kind of irregularity when occupancy was rather temporary, and people were eager to move father west.

In such a situation, it is not hard to imagine the same person having two or more warrants, and perhaps not living on either of them. There were even cases of two people with a warrant for the same land. So it may not be too surprising that John Schrock bought a part of Christian Speicher's original warrant in Brothers Valley, while Joseph, one of Christian, Sr.'s, sons, moved to Stony Creek Township. Perhaps the two brothers-in-law had some kind of understanding by which John and Maria Schrock preferred to live nearer the Miller homestead.

We know that Isaac Miller's wife shortly was remarried to Joseph Forney, who probably already had a farm. Their children were young enough that they were given guardians through the Orphans Court. The guardians were without

---

[153] She was the youngest daughter (born ca1770), according to *AAMG*.

exception members of the Dunkards. For the disposal of the property of 100 acres, the court ordered it to be equally divided between the widow and the children. "Twelve honest men [sic]" were chosen to carry this out. Joseph Speicher already had some land next to the Isaac Miller farm, and since he and several other neighbors and relatives were among the twelve, it was only natural that Joseph added this farm to his own, and the proceeds helped support the orphans.

It must have happened over and over. The ones who stayed took over the lands of those who wanted to leave, if only to provide for the future of their children. Joseph and Elizabeth must have wondered whether their own children would want to stay in Pennsylvania. Of course, land was plentiful and was not such a great investment of money as it is now. It appears that Joseph and Elizabeth remained with the Amish-Mennonite Church, although they were surrounded by members of the Brethren in Stony Creek Township. The Christian Yoder family, who were church leaders among the Glades Amish, also lived in Stony Creek Township, but on the west side of Stony Creek.

At least three marriages took place between the family of Christian Yoder, the pioneer in Somerset County, and children of Joseph Speicher. Others married into Amish families or moved to Amish communities further north. It is interesting to note that the descendants of Joseph moved to other Amish communities, while Christian, his brother's children, and grandchildren moved to United Brethren communities, even though they were married to sisters. As far as it is known, Joseph and Elizabeth lived on their farm in Stony Creek Township until they died.

Joseph, as noted above, had a small plat in Stony Creek Township, as it appeared just north of the farm of Isaac Miller. A closer examination of the actual plat map in the Somerset Courthouse shows it to be rather just south of the Isaac Miller property (forty-four acres), which would make it between the original Speicher land and the land of John Miller, Sr. Since John Miller and Joseph Speicher were both among the "twelve honest men" to assess the property of Isaac Miller, it may indicate that they wished to take over some of the Isaac Miller property, since Joseph had, at first, only forty-four acres. The Christian Speicher property was only surveyed and warranted officially in 1809, and could have been a situation similar to that of John Miller, Sr., who only had it surveyed in order to transfer it to someone else. In the case of Christian Speicher, it may have meant that he was selling it and moving to Ohio. This may indicate why John Schrock was able to buy a piece of land from his brother-in-law. Joseph, in turn, took over the Isaac Miller farm. [154]

---

[154] Courthouse records, Somerset Co., Pa.

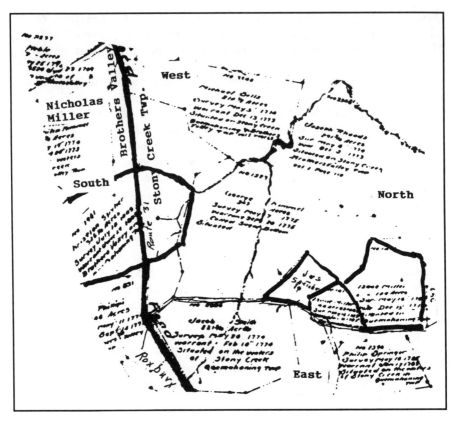

From the plat maps of Stony Creek and Brothers Valley, showing plats of Joseph Speicher, Christian Speicher, Isaac Miller, and Nicholas Miller. John Miller, Sr.'s farm is south of Christian Speicher's farm.

The Children of Elizabeth Miller and Joseph Speicher

1. **Christian Speicher**, born ca1788; as the oldest son, lived on the home farm of his parents. His wife's name is not known. They had three known children, a daughter and two sons, Henry and Jacob. This is not yet proven, but the census records seem to confirm this, since there is a Henry Speicher, age thirty-one, wife Huldah, age twenty-five, and a son Jonathan, age one, in Stony Creek Township in 1850.[155] According to *AAMG*, Jacob, Christian's son, may have lived in Shade Township.[156]
2. **Elizabeth Speicher**, born 1790; died 1874; married Joseph Yoder. They lived in Conemaugh Township. They had five sons and two daughters. Their son

---

[155] 1850 Census records.
[156] *AAMG*.

Isaac was married to Susanna Mishler, daughter of Christian Mishler, son of Elizabeth Speicher's sister (?Susanna) and Christian Mishler.

3. **Jacob Spiker**, born ca1792; married and lived with his wife in Tuscarawas County, Ohio. She was under thirty years old in 1830, according to the census record, so she was born ca1801.[157] They had four sons in 1830. The reason for the conclusion that this is the right Jacob is that in the census, Jacob Spiker is listed between Jacob Miller, Sr., and Jacob Miller, Jr., who were the first Amish-Mennonite ministers in Ohio, and they were the uncle and cousin of Jacob Spiker, if he is the son of Joseph Speicher.
4. **Tobias Speicher**, born 1798; died 1876; married 1) Mary ___, born 1798; died 1874; married 2) Sarah ___, born 1821; died 1909; no children. They lived in Stony Creek Township.
5. **Mary Speicher**, born 1794; died 1860; married (David Blough?) as his second wife. They moved to Milton Township, Wayne County, Ohio. David had seven children from his first wife, and Mary and David had five sons.
6. **Joseph Speicher, Jr.**, was born 1797; died 1862; married 1) Anna Lehman, born 1803; died 1845. He married 2) Rebecca Musser, born 1829; died 1892. They lived for a while in Jenner Township, but by 1850 they were living in Garrett County, Maryland. They probably belonged to the Church of the Brethren, considering the names of the families their children married into. In his first marriage, Joseph and his wife had two sons and two daughters who grew to maturity. In his second marriage, they had three sons and three daughters who had families, and a single daughter.[158]
7. **Solomon Speicher**, born 1800; died 1882; married Elizabeth Blough, born 1798; died 1869; niece of his sister Mary's husband, David Blough. They lived in Stony Creek Township until 1840, according to the census, and then moved to Garrett County, Maryland, where they were living in 1850. They had five sons and four daughters. According to the names of the families into which their children married, they must have been at least partly members of the Church of the Brethren.[159]
8. **Abraham Speicher**, listed as a son of Joseph and Elizabeth Speicher, but nothing has been found of him or his family.
9. **Sarah Speicher**, born 1818; died 1879; married three times. Married 1) Stephen Yoder, born 1812; died 1850; they had three sons and four daughter; married 2) Peter Hostetler, a minister, born 1807; died 1863; no children; m. 3) Tobias W. Yoder, born 1810; died 1893; no children. Amish-Mennonite Church.[160]

---

[157] 1850 census, Tuscarawas Co., Ohio.
[158] 1850 census, Allegany Co., Md.
[159] *Ibid.*
[160] List of children from *AAMG*. Census.

Other Amish-Mennonite Families in Europe and America

What about the other Miller families included by Dr. Gingerich in *AAMG*, you may well ask, since I indicated in the first part of this book that there are some that should not be in the same family as John Miller, Sr. I already pointed out that the Christian Miller who came to America in 1742 is nowhere mentioned in *AAMG*. I think that at least half of those shown as siblings of John Miller, Sr., including the Christian who married Freny (Veronica) Gnaegi, should be in the family of Cumru Christian, from the family of the Daniel Miller, whose descendants thought that since Daniel was the son of Christian, then Daniel should be the father's name. They looked in the ship lists and found a Daniel who came in 1750, just about the right time, but he seemed to have come alone, or at least not with others with Amish names, as on several previous ships.

Gingerich rightly rejects this logic, since a will filed in Reading shows the same children for the Christian of the will as for those of the supposed Daniel.[161] I have suggested for some time that since Johannes Gnaegi came on the 1742 ship with the other Christian Miller, it is logical to connect the two, but one generation before; and Christian Miller, Sr.'s, wife perhaps was Johannes Gnaegi's sister, rather than his daughter. Johannes Gnaegi himself married the sister of one of the passengers named Yoder, as his second wife.[162]

Isaac Miller (ML8) might be thought to be a son of the above Christian. But the fact that he settled near John and Nicholas Miller in Stony Creek Township and negotiated with Joseph Speicher over land makes me want to make him a younger brother of John, Sr., and Nicholas. I am not sure about Abraham (ML7), but his movements are those of the Cumru group. I have no documents to prove or disprove this. I also indicated I would place MLD, who lived his whole life in Upper Bern Township, at least that part in America, so I would put him in the Bern Township group or the "Jacob" family. There is also a Jacob whom *AAMG* does not mention at all. He moved with the John Miller family, along with his son Michael, settling in southern Somerset County in what would be Summit Township today.

Among the others, MLB, MLE, and MLG clearly seem to have been with the Brethren from the start. Christian (MLB) was a Brethren deacon; (MLE)

---

[161] Discussed by C. Z. Mast in *Annals of the Conestoga Valley* (1942).
[162] Eugene F. Kenaga, *Descendants of Johannes Gnäge* (1988).

Peter settled near Pocahontas, which was Brethren territory. MLG lived in Elklick or Summit Township, and the marriages of his children appear to be to families of that group. But some of the children of Amish parents joined the Brethren. That is true, but it is possible to trace the original Brethren families to communities further east. Most of the Brethren were converts in America, but a study of ship lists shows that those who were already or had become Brethren also came in groups on immigrant ships, usually ten or more years before the first Amish. MLF and MLH did marry Amish wives and came a bit later. A larger migration from Alsace, Baden, and Hesse came after 1800 and included some Amish-Mennonite Millers. They were usually not closely related to our Millers, so we confine ourselves to those who were originally Amish.

The reason for favoring the Palatinate as the last place where the eighteenth century Amish-Mennonite immigrants came from was that it was their last place of refuge. However, even though the rulers there wanted them as farmers, they were barely tolerated. Some of the families were there only temporarily until they could go to a place that was more tolerant. A group passed through Alsace and the Palatinate to Waldeck in Hesse, where they remained fairly peacefully until about 1850. Even then they left, so that there are no more Amish or Mennonites in Hesse or Waldeck today.

If that is so, why are there still Anabaptists in Switzerland and Alsace today? At first they made use of places of refuge as near to their former homes as possible. First was the bishopric of Basel where Henry Muller and Christian Knagey had settled, as discussed in the historical introduction. Next was Neuchatel, now a French-speaking canton of Switzerland which was then under the rule of Prussia. It was the same for Montbeliard, which was not a part of France then. Although French-speaking, it was ruled by the German state of Württemberg. After Alsace became a part of France, they might have emigrated to any of those places, at least for a while.

The majority of Mennonites in Switzerland today are living in the Jura Mountain region, which was once in the bishopric of Basel. Then there was the little principality of Salm, not yet absorbed by the French, and a few families went there. That left the Palatinate, which at that time was ruled by Bavaria, since there was no central German government. A part was ruled by the Duchy of Zweibrücken, which overlapped with the Palatinate in places; for example, Mülhofen, where we think the Müllers may have lived, was ruled by the dukes of Pfalz-Zweibrücken (Palatinate, Zweibrücken Duchy), so they are not in the Palatinate Mennonite census lists.

The French Revolution declared that all men are equal, so it is easier to locate Anabaptists after 1789, because all citizens had to be registered by the state. For the Revolutionary French, citizenship meant that the citizens should also fight for France. One of their first moves was to occupy all of Alsace, including enclaves such as Salm and Montbeliard. Then they proceeded to invade the Palatinate and other parts of Germany, and the Anabaptists lost their military exemption. Napoleon came along and deposed rulers right and left, and soon the conscripts were expected to fight in his wars in all parts of Europe,

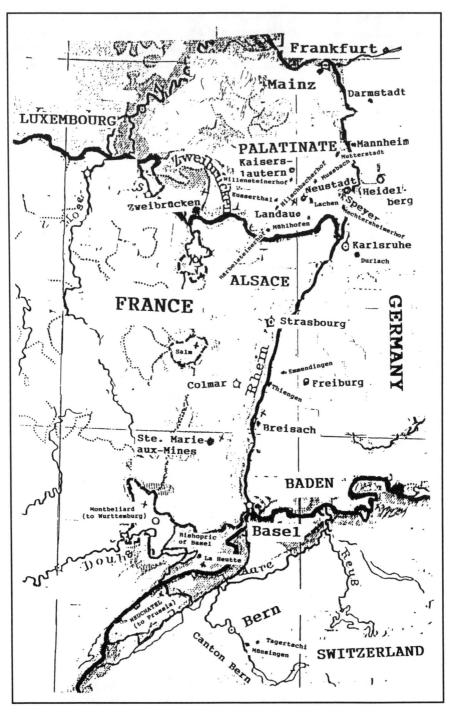

Map showing the places the Millers lived in Europe and routes of migration, also the places of refuge.

including Russia. That is another story and did not concern those who emigrated before 1790. Naturally for Amish and Mennonites, this was an intolerable situation and it caused a new emigration from Europe. These are some of the problems this group of people had to face. Yet some remained quietly in their homes, as many of the young men escaped the draft and came to America. Others can be found in many of their former homes, but it is only a remnant.

Amish-Mennonites in the Palatinate in the 1700s

1. Adam Kurtz - 1713
   Jakob Kurtz
   Claus Müller - 1723
   Jakob Müller
   Jakob Holly - 1732
   Johann Müller - 1756
   All Mühlhofen [163]

2. Christian Holly - 1718
   Hans Ringenberg - 1748
   Isaak Hochstettler - 1770
   Hans Rupp - 1783
   Johannes Esch
   Johannes Maurer
   Bärbelsteinerhof [164]

3. Jakob Müller - 1749
   Mörzheim [165]

4. Jost Joder
   Lachen - 1717
   Johannes Joder
   Mussbach - 1738

5. Johannes Knegi
   Mutterstadt - 1724

6. Michael Müller - 1743
   Christian Müller
   (left for the new land)
   Hilschbacherhof

7. Christen Zoug - 1720
   Willensteinerhof
   nr. Trippstadt
   s. Kaiserslautern

8. Johannes Nafziger - 1738
   Christian Bürcky
   Abraham Kurtz
   Jacob Kurtz
   Mechtersheimerhof
   near Speyer

9. Casper Schrag
   Ulrich Schrag - 1728
   Nicholas Stoltzfus - 1744
   Johann Martin Bornträger - 1750
   Zweibrücken [166]

10. Ulrich Mischler
    Hans Mischler
    Hans Hürzeler
    Jacob Kurtz [167]
    (Baden-Durlach) - 1729
    (probably also Ulrich Speicher)

---

[163] Speyer Archives, Temporalbestand.
[164] *Pirmasenser Geschichtsblätter*, 1938.
[165] *Palatine Mennonite Census Lists*.
[166] Drumm, op. cit.
[167] J. Virgil Miller, "An Update on Mishlers, etc.," *MFH*, Jan. 1996.

Amish-Mennonites in Berks County in the Northkill (N) and Cumru (C) Settlements[168]

1. Jacob Miller (N)
   Ulrich Speicher (N)
   Abraham Miller (?)
   Christian Miller (N)
   Ulrich Speicher (N)
   Benedict Lehman (N)
   Charming Nancy - Oct. 8, 1737

2. Jacob Hochstetler (N)
   Charming Nancy, Nov. 9, 1738

3. Christian Jotter (N)
   Jacob (X) Yoder (N)
   Christian Yoder (N)
   Johannes Qnäg (Gnaegi/Knegi) (N)
   Moritz Zug (N)
   Christian Zug (N)
   Johannes Zug (N)
   Christian Miller (C)
   Jacob Kurtz (C)
   Frances & Elizabeth, Sept. 21, 1742

4. Hans (+) Kurtz (N)
   Stephen (+) Kurtz (N)
   Muscliffe Galley, Dec. 22, 1744

5. Hannes Miller (N)
   Jacob Misseler (C)
   Josep Mischle (C)
   Mattheis Nafzger (N)
   Benedict Leman (N)
   Abraham Kurtz (C)
   Ulrich Mischler (C)
   Phoenix, Sept. 15, 1749

6. Nikel Stoltzfus (C)
   Christian Stoltzfus (C)
   Johannes Schrag
   Polly, Oct. 23, 1766

7. Martin Bornträger
   Sally, Oct. 5, 1767

---

[168] Strassburger and Hinke, ship lists.

Some Statistics and Interesting Facts About the Family of John Miller, Sr.

1. John Miller, Sr., the subject of this history, had eleven children, five boys and six girls. He had ninety-two grandchildren.
2. In the first three generations of my line (John Miller, Jr.), there were eleven children born to each: John Miller, Sr., John Miller, Jr., and Yost Miller, the pioneer in Holmes County, Ohio. But, in the first generation, all eleven raised families; in the second, nine of the eleven raised families, and two died young; in the third generation in Ohio, of the eleven children of Yost Miller, only four grew up to raise families.
3. Of the eleven children of John Miller, Sr., Catherine Miller and her husband, Jacob Kauffman, had the most children, thirteen who all raised families, and had the most grandchildren, 111.
4. John Miller, Sr., had ninety-two grandchildren (over eight per family). He had 617 great-grandchildren (6.7 per family).
5. In the family of John Miller, Jr., the parents died in Pennsylvania, but all eleven children moved to Ohio.
6. David Miller, son of John Miller, Jr., had fourteen sons and one daughter, but his older sister Barbara's daughter, Catherine, had one son and eleven daughters.
7. In the family of Jacob Miller, the parents and three of the four sons moved to Ohio, while one son, Benedict, stayed in Pennsylvania and was a minister and bishop in the Amish-Mennonite Church.
8. In the family of Peter Miller, his son, Moses P. Miller, moved to Ohio and became a minister and bishop in the Amish-Mennonite Church. When the division came about 1860 between the Old Order Amish and the Amish who became more modern and built churches, Moses (who was called "Gross Mose") became a leader in that church. His nephew, Moses J. Miller, who was called "Klein Mose," became a leader in the Old Order Amish. He was the son of Gross Mose's brother Jonas, who also chose the Old Order. Gross Mose was called that name not because he was big, but because when they were children, he was older. Because their names were both Mose, the older one was called "Gross" and the younger one "Glee Mose," as the Amish say.
9. The family of John Miller, Sr., were pioneers. The first Amish settler in Tuscarawas County, Ohio, was Jacob Miller, his wife Anna, and his sons John, Henry, and Jacob. In nearby Holmes County, Ohio, of the first four families to come, three were children of Peter Miller: Magdalena, Sarah, and

The family of Yost B. Miller, Berlin, Ohio, grandson of Yost Miller the pioneer (Yost B. Miller not in picture). Taken from Oscar Miller's book Yost B. Miller Family History, 1976.

Jonas. Moses, the youngest brother, came later and became a minister. Of the first four Amish families to come to Indiana, two of the four were sons of Joseph Miller: Daniel and Joseph. Joseph became a minister and bishop in Indiana.

10. Three of the children of Christian Speicher, Sr., married children of John Miller, Sr.: Joseph married Barbara Speicher, his first wife; Freny married Christian Speicher, Jr.; and Elizabeth married Joseph Speicher.

11. The family of Jacob Miller, son of John, Sr., had a long line of ministers and bishops: Jacob was a minister and bishop in Somerset County, Pennsylvania. His son Benedict was a minister and bishop in Somerset County. Then Benedict's son, Joel B. Miller, did the same, followed by his son, Joel J. Miller. Joel J.'s son, Jonas B. Miller, was a minister and editor of the church paper *Herold der Wahrheit*. Jonas's brother, Alvin J. Miller, was one the first leaders of Mennonite Relief services after World War I, in the organization that became the Mennonite Central Committee. Ivan J. Miller continued the line of ministers and bishops, living in Grantsville, Maryland. His son David is working with Rosedale Missions at Irwin, Ohio.

12. Even homesteads can travel. When Bishop Benedict Miller died, his retirement house was used as an out-building for many years. Through the efforts of Dr. Alta Schrock of Spruce Forest Village, the house was moved from across the border in Somerset County, Pennsylvania, to its present site near Grantsville, Maryland. The house now serves to remind people of the heritage that Benedict Miller represents.

13. My ancestor Yost Miller was in the same lot for minister as Benedict Miller. Destiny decreed (or was it the Lord's leading?) that Yost went to Ohio and Benedict stayed in Pennsylvania. Otherwise, all of Benedict's descendants would have lived in Ohio and beyond, and my ancestors all would have stayed in Pennsylvania! It hardly works that way. Yost also led a useful life, if a bit more secular. When his father died suddenly at the age of fifty in 1802, his sons Yost and David, ages twenty-seven and twenty-three, were the young executors of their father's will. This was good apprenticeship for what he later did—helped numerous people to settle their estates, and helped with inheritance and property problems. The first township meeting in Walnut Creek Township, Holmes County, was held at his home in 1823 for the election of offices. He was also a member of the first board of school examiners in Holmes County, Ohio, according to the *DJH*.[169]

---

[169] *DJH*, #9155, pp. 955-956.

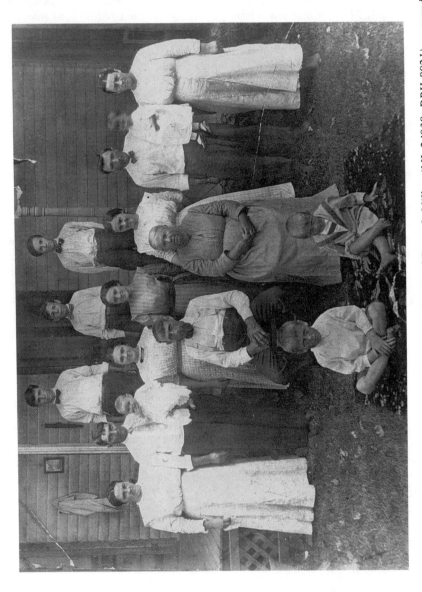

Typical families of Millers in Holmes County, Ohio. Above is the family of Peter J. Miller, (ML 24938, DBH 8921), a grandson of Gross Mose Miller, of the family of Peter. Address: Shanesville, Ohio. Nine children: five daughters and four sons. Courtesy: Vernon D. Miller, Ohio.

How You and I Are Descended From John Miller, Sr.

	MY LINE		YOUR LINE
I.	John Miller, Sr. (ca1730-1798)	I.	John Miller, Sr. (ca1730-1798)
II.	John Miller, Jr. (1752-1802)	II.	_____
III.	Yost Miller (1776-1846)	III.	_____
IV.	Benjamin J. Miller (1813-1877)	IV.	_____
V.	Daniel B. Miller (1838-1928)	V.	_____
VI.	Benjamin D. Miller (1860-1932)	VI.	_____
VII.	Ura R. Miller (1897-1980)	VII.	_____
VIII.	James Virgil Miller (b. 1924)	VIII.	_____
IX.		IX.	_____
X.		X.	_____

Appendix No. I

Family of John Miller*

9146. **John Miller**, who was wounded by the Indians when they were taking the family of Jacob Hostetler into captivity, moved later to Somerset County, where he died. Moses B. Miller, Geistown, Pennsylvania, wrote an account of John's family. This account follows, supplemented by material furnished by William F. Hochstetler of family 2228. Jacob, 9147; John, 9154; Christian, 9162; Peter, 9163; Joseph, 9169; Mrs. Joseph Speicher, of Somerset County, Pennsylvania; Mrs. Christian Speicher, of Somerset County, Pennsylvania; Mrs. Jacob Kauffman, 9173; Mrs. Christian Mishler, 9174; Mrs. John Schrag, whose children appear in family 2863; Barbara, wife of Jacob Hochstetler, whose descendants are given in families 3-1386.

9147. **Jacob Miller**, 9146, married Anna Stutzman, who was born April 12, 1755. They moved to Ohio about 1808-9. An account of his moving appears in the *Mennonite Year Book* of 1909. He was a minister in the Amish Church and preached what was probably the first sermon in Holmes County. In the spring of 1808, Bishop Jacob Miller, with his sons Henry and Jacob, came to Ohio and entered a section of land, about a mile northeast of Sugarcreek, Ohio. After assisting his sons build cabins and start farming, he returned to Somerset County, Pennsylvania, and the next spring moved his family to Ohio, bringing with him Jonas Stutzman, a nephew of his wife, who became the first settler on Walnut Creek. John, 9148; Benedict, 9150; Henry, 9152; Jacob, 9153.

9147. May 6, 1810, four young Amish families joined Jonas Stutzman on Walnut Creek. Jonas Miller and his wife Catherine Hershberger, of family 9167; Christian Yoder and his wife Magdalena Hershberger, sister of Catherine (see family 4569, note, and family 2351); Joseph Mast and his wife Sarah Miller, sister of Jonas Miller of family 9167; and John Troyer and wife Magdalena Miller, also sister of Jonas Miller.

---

*Note: Taken from the 1977 reprint of *Descendants of Jacob Hochstetler*. This passage is from the Appendix, pp. 953-959. It was originally written by Moses B. Miller of Geistown, Pa., with additional notes by William F. Hochstetler, author of the historical introduction to the history.

9148. **John J. Miller**, 9147, was the first in his neighborhood to use a letter in his name to distinguish him from others of the same name, and was much ridiculed for it, being called Jay Miller. He moved from Maryland to Ohio in 1811, entered land in Section 16, Walnutcreek Township, Holmes County, Ohio, which he sold in 1816 to Yost Miller. He then entered a quarter section near Barrs Mills, Ohio, where he built the first mill in the vicinity. In 1848 he sold a lot in Walnutcreek to Jacob D. Miller. He was twice married, both wives signing their names to deeds as Catherine. Mrs. Elizabeth Richardson, Shanesville, Ohio, of family 4697, thinks the first wife was Catherine Hochstetler of family 3061. Daughter died when grown, buried near Barrs Mills; Solomon; Mary, married Jacob Biddle; Adam, 9149; Mrs. Correll; Mrs. Schritchfield; Mrs. Joseph Gorden. Married 2) Catherine Willard, widow of Mr. Ehrich, daughter of Henry Willard. About 1850, John J. Miller, with his wife and three youngest children, moved to Miami County, Indiana; Rebecca, married Levi Weibel; Absalom, married Barbara Schrock, of family 1726, note; Enoch, married Elizabeth Lehman.

9149. **Adam Miller**, 9148, Chicago, Illinois, at death; was born in 1810 and lived to be over ninety years old. He married in 1835, Phoebe F. Talmadge of Knox County, Ohio. In early life he left the Amish Church and joined the Methodist Church. He gives an account of change of church life in a little book entitled *Hostetler*, or *The Mennonite Boy Converted by a Methodist Preacher*, published in 1848 at New York by Carleton and Power, Sunday School Union. He speaks of his birth in 1810, moving when six months of age to Ohio, where his mother died in his ninth year. He speaks of four children older than himself. He wrote several works and was quite prominent in his church, having engaged in mission work in Baltimore, New York, West Virginia, Indiana, and Ohio.

9150. **Benedict Miller**, 9147, lived in Somerset County, Pennsylvania. He was born November 10, 1781; died June 1837; married July 17, 1803, Catherine Beachy, who was born November 20, 1778; died September 24, 1834; the daughter of Peter Bitsche and Sally Blauman. He was ordained bishop in the Amish Church on Whit-Monday, 1813. *Beachy Genealogy* families 298-419. (A) Henry, April 23, 1804-February 28, 1824; (B) Peter, June 17, 1805-July 29, 1879; married Catherine Yoder, born May 26, 1808-September 10, 1883; (C) Mary, of family 5976; (D) Saloma, June 12, 1808-March 12, 1885; married John Kempf of family 1637; (E) Catherine, January 15, 1810-July 1852; married William Bender; (F) Joel, March 27, 1811-August 2, 1885; married Catherine Brenneman; (G) Susanna, October 5, 1812-July 25, 1889; married D. P. Guengerich; (H) Elizabeth, November 9, 1813—deceased; married Isaac Eash, deceased; the family of their daughter Catherine appears in family 3016; (I) Benedict, May 20, 1815-October 23, 1883; married Barbara Guengerich; (J) Barbara, January 5, 1817-October 27, 1864; married Jacob Guengerich, of families 4483, 5141, 5145, 5558; (K) Moses B., September 4, 1819-___; married Sarah Hershberger, of families 2519, 3342, 3877; (L) Jacob B., November 11, 1821-October 26, 1875; married Anna Schambrick. Benedict

Miller married 2) Catherine Ashe, widow of Mr. Keim, and she later married Peter Livengood. (M) Lydia, married Sim Miller; (N) Magdalena, 9151.

9151. **Magdalena Miller**, 9150, Kalona, Iowa, at death; was born August 1837; died February 5, 1910; married John J. Miller, who died January 25, 1890. (A) Lucy, died April 21, 1891; married Stephen Yoder, who died April 12, 1908; (B) Peter, died April 3, 1891; married Mary Laymon; (C) Joseph, married Mary Bender, of family 4122; (D) Joel, married Amelia Yoder; (E) John, married Barbara Yoder, of family 5370; (F) Catherine, married Daniel Gingerich; (G) Magdalena, married John Hershberger; (H) Mary, married John Knepp; (I) Anna, died April 20, 1898; married Jacob Brenneman, of family 3135; (J) Manassas, married Mary Yoder, of family 1651; (K) Benedict, married Mary Miller; (L) Elizabeth, Centralia, Missouri; married John Yoder. The post office address of all above is Kalona, Iowa.

9152. **Henry Miller**, 9147, lived in Ohio. His children are: (A) Zachariah, married Gertrude Hostetler, of family 4671; (B) Daniel, married Judith Gindelsperger; (C) Elizabeth, wife of Joseph Summers, of Washington County, Iowa, of family 9168; (D) Catherine, wife of Elias Carvel; (E) Benedict, married Catherine Gindelsperger; (F) Judith, wife of Adam Kreider; (G) Magdalena, wife of Jacob Yoder; (H) Barbara, wife of Jacob D. Yoder; (I) Eva, wife of Jacob Shanover; (J) Jacob, married Sally Troyer; (K) Levi, married 1) Miss Olds, of Summit County, Ohio; married 2) Catherine Bale; (L) Dorothea, married Christian Welti; died early in Saltcreek Township, Holmes County, Ohio; no children.

9153. **Jacob Miller**, 9147, lived in Ohio. His children are: Susannah, wife of Christian Grabill; Barbara, wife of Isaac Hochstetler, of family 1666; Catherine, wife of Moses D. Yoder; Eli, married Veronica Hooley; Eva, wife of Moses Hochstetler, of family 5516; Isaac, married Lydia Troyer, of family 4480; Veronica, wife of Jacob S. Yoder; Elizabeth, wife of Noah Mast, of family 4002; Rebecca, who died single.

9154. **John Miller**, 9146, moved to Ohio about 1815 and located in the southeast part of German Township, Holmes County, but later moved to Berlin Township. His name is generally written John, but it really was Annas, the same name that appers in John 18:13. (A) Yost, 9155; (B) Daniel, 9156; (C) David, 9158; (D) Catherine, February 14, 1783-February 20, 1843; married Benjamin Hochstetler, of family 1665; (E) Jacob, 9159; (F) John or Annas, February 16, 1787-February 16, 1867; married Anna Gnaegi, of *Gnagey Genealogy* families 3-64; see families 6496, note, 4468, 4627; (G) Elizabeth,

9154. Solomon Miller was assisting his brother Isaac cut down a tree, and was caught and severely injured, dying within a few days. As there were no sawmills in the settlement previous to 1818, it was necessary to make a coffin of hewn boards, joined with pegs. His death occurred in 1815-16. Hans Troyer, one of the first settlers, and Rebecca, wife of Jacob Holderman, residing on what was later the David Gerber farm, were the first grown persons to die in the settlement and were buried in the same way.

March 16, 1789-deceased; married Moses Beachy, the first Amish couple to marry in Holmes County, Ohio, of *Beachy Genealogy* families 69-191; (H) Isaac, 9160; (I) Emanuel, 9161; (J) Solomon, November 10, 1795; killed by a falling tree; (K) Elias, June 22, 1798; died rather young; unmarried.

9155. **Yost Miller**, 9154, was born January 19, 1776; died May 12, 1846, and married Gertraut Yoder. He was well educated for his time and did much business as executor, administrator, and guardian, both while residing in Pennsylvania, and after his removal to Ohio. He was executor of the will of John Hochstetler of family 1387, in 1813 in Pennsylvania, and also for the estate of Joseph Hochstetler of family 4451, in Ohio in 1823. The first township meeting was held at his house in 1825 for the election of officers in Walnutcreek Township. He was also a member of the first board of school examiners for Holmes County Amish Church. (A) Sarah, July 7, 1802; married Peter Schrag, a minister of Wayne County, Ohio; see Smith's *Mennonites in America*, page 218; (B) Jonathan, January 15, 1804-died single; (C) Isaac, September 6, 1806; died young; (D) Susanna, October 28, 1808-1884; a dwarf; unmarried; (E) Elias, November 28, 1810-deceased; married Barbara Hershberger; (F) Benjamin, April 28, 1813-May 13, 1877; married Mary Mast, of family 5058; (G) Michael, May 28, 1816-died single; (H) Yost, September 14, 1818-died single; (I) Magdalena, August 20, 1820-died single; (J) Solomon, November 3, 1821-___; married Magdalena Kauffman; (K) Elizabeth, d. in infancy. He married 2) Maria Folmer, of family 4161.

9156. **Daniel Miller**, 9154, was born February 5, 1778; died July 16, 1858; and married Magdalena Troyer. He moved to Ohio in 1815, near Baltic, and later near Berlin, on the farm now owned by Christian Miller, a grandson. (A) Tobias, 9157; (B) Michael, April 28, 1805-died young; (C) Susanna, February 8, 1806-July 25, 1882; married Christian Borntreger, of family 9144; (D) Moses, May 25, 1807-___; married 1) Sarah Troyer; married 2) Barbara Haage, whose father was a noted minister from the Old Country, of families 3938, 4009, 5754; (E) Michael, September 5, 1809; died young; (F) Aaron, December 12, 1810; mute; died from a gunshot; (G) Joseph, February 20, 1813-___; married Elizabeth Sommers and had three children; (H) Benjamin, October 1, 1813; married Susan Yoder; had three children; was killed by a falling tree; (I) Rebecca, October 20, 1817-April 1877; married Jacob Hostetler, of family 2075; (J) Eva, August 13, 1819; died young, feebleminded.

9157. **Tobias Miller**, 9156, was born August 6, 1801, and by his first wife had children: (A) Moses T., married Elizabeth Yoder, of family 6422; (B) Elizabeth, married Samuel Hochstetler of family 5689; (C) Daniel; died single; lame; (D) Christian, Berlin, Ohio, married Elizabeth Mast, daughter of Abraham Mast and Fanny Kurtz; (E) Lydia, died young; (F) John, married 1) Catherine Mast; married 2) Fanny Zook; married 3) Fanny Speicher; (G) David, married Mill Skilling; (H) Jacob, married Lydia Wenger; (I) Stephen, married 1) Catherine Degler; married 2) Leah Wenger. Tobias m. 2) Nancy Hochstetler, of family 6400; (J) Aaron T., of family 6434.

9158. **David Miller**, 9154, was born October 2, 1779, and married Elizabeth Troyer. He resided on a farm in Walnutcreek Township, Holmes County, Ohio, while his brother Jacob resided on an adjoining farm in German Township. It is on the line between these farms that some of the early Millers, notably young Solomon, are buried. (A) Jonas, March 1, 1805-___; married Veronica Miller; (B) Daniel, September 23, 1806; married Catherine Weaver, of families 5060, 5170, 5175, 5186; (C) Stephen, February 12, 1808-___; married Barbara Mishler; (D) Michael, April 21, 1809-___; married 1) Mary Mast; married 2) Susanna Mast, of family 5197; (E) Noah, December 26, 1810-___; married Veronica Hershberger, of family 5412; (F) David, May 4, 1812-___; married Magdalena Mishler, of family 3775, note; (G) Yost, March 20, 1814-___; married Veronica Gerber; (H) Jacob, May 14, 1816-May 15, 1897; married 1) Veronica Mast of family 5135; (I) Simon, May 14, 1816-___, of families 1939, 5233, 5237; married Anna Miller, who married 2) Shem Miller, of families 9161, 4393, 4851; (J) Elizabeth, January 1818-October 3, 1890; married Jonas Hochstetler, of family 6139; (K) Benjamin, September 3, 1819-___; married Veronica Mast; (L) Moses, March 19, 1822-1835; (M) Andrew, September 13, 1828-1849; it is claimed that the old family record had at least two more sons, one of whom was named Joseph.

9159. **Jacob Miller**, 9154, was born December 14, 1784; died 1830; and was buried on Easter Monday. He married Veronica Troyer. (A) Elizabeth, married Jacob Kauffman; (B) Magdalena, married Peter S. Weaver; (C) Veronica, married Isaac D. Miller, son of Daniel Miller, of family 1939, note, and families 1484, 5719; (D) Judith, died single; deformed; (E) Jonas, married Catherine J. Miller; (F) Eva, married Benedict Mullet of families 3199, 5220, 5224, 5697; (G) Daniel, married (1) Rachel A. Miller, of family 1939, note; married 2) Mary Garver; married 3) Mrs. Mary (Hershberger) Yutzy; married 4) Leah Hershberger, widow of Joseph Keim; see family 4390; (H) John, married 1) Magdalena Miller, daughter of Daniel Miller, of family 1939, note; see families 4585, 5603; 5702; married 2) Elizabeth Stutzman, widow of Solomon Eash; no children; (I) Mary, married Emanuel Miller, son of Henry Miller, of family 1939, note.

9157. Abraham Mast of Mast Genealogy Family 1557. Fanny Kurtz, daughter of Joseph Kurtz and Fanny Miller, of family 3062, note. The children of Abraham and Fanny Mast are: Susanna, born November 12, 1826-___; married John Yoder, who died in 1909; Fanny, May 21, 1829-February 18, 1892; married Jacob Yoder; Elizabeth; Mary, July 17, 1837-February 11, 1908; married Eli D. Miller; Sarah, born August 11, 1834-___; married Isaac Hertzler of Hertzler Genealogy Family 119; Rebecca, May 14, 1840-September 6, 1886; married Moses J. Miller; Catherine, born 1843-October 27, 1865; married John Miller, see above. The second wife of Abraham Mast was Elizabeth Kurtz, a sister of his first wife.

9160. **Isaac Miller**, 9154, was born April 9, 1791; died September 18, 1874; and married 1) Mary Yoder. (A) Magdalena, married John Borntrager of Lagrange Country, Indiana, of family 9118; (B) Solomon, died at ninety-two years, an Amish minister; married 1) Elizabeth Brenneman; married 2) Miss Yoder; (C) Yost, died at eighty-six years; married Mary Schmucker of family 3186, note, with whom he had seventeen children, of family 3110.1. Married 2) Catherine Beachy. (D) Dinah, married Abraham Weaver, of families 2104 and 3122; (E) Peter, married Catherine Miller, daughter of Jonas Miller, of families 9167, 4541; (F) Sarah, married Simon Keck; no children; (G) Isaac, married Polly Frey, of families 7692, 5191; (H) Catherine, married Isaac H. Miller, son of Henry Miller, of family 1939, note; no children; (I) Emanuel, married Susanna Mast, of family 5197. Married 3) Polly Mosser. (J) Mary, married Peter P. Hershberger, of families 4388, 5353, 5533; (K) Barbara, married William Weaver; (L) Susanna, married William Weaver, as his second wife.

9161. **Emanuel Miller**, 9154, was born February 2, 179_; died December 4, 1848; married Elizabeth Yoder, of family 4135, note. Their children: (A) Jacob, married Elizabeth Hershberger; daughter of Christian Hershberger, of family 4569, note; (B) Mary, married Christian Hershberger, brother of Elizabeth Hershberger, preceding; Christian Hershberger married 2) Elizabeth Hochstetler, of family 4383; he married 3) Miss Yoder; (C) John, married Sarah Stutzman, of families 4444, 5536; (D) Elizabeth, married Abraham Beachy, of *Beachy Genealogy* family 435; (E) Shem, an Amish bishop, married Mrs. Anna Miller, daughter of Jonathan Miller, of family 1939, note; Anna's first husband was Simon Miller, of family 1939, note, and family 9158; (F) William, married Susannah Mast, of family 3939.

9162. **Christian Miller**, 9146, lived in "The Glades," Stony Creek Township, Somerset County, Pennsylvania; Solomon; Peter; Mrs. Gindelsperger; Mrs. Kauffman of Tuscarora Valley, Pennsylvania; Annie, died single.

9163. **Peter Miller**, 9146, Meyersdale, Pennsylvania; married Miss Stutzman, of family 9190. (A) Abraham, June 15, 1780-deceased; married Miss Lichty; (B) Magdalena, November 13, 1781-deceased; married John Troyer, one of four first families in Walnutcreek Township; (C) Peter, 9164; (D) Jonas, 9167; (E) Joseph, December 1, 1789-___; (F) Jeremiah, June 26, 1792-deceased; married 1) Miss Leibengut, who died from burns; he resided in Fairfield County, Ohio, where he had a distillery; later he moved to Washington County, Iowa, where he married 2) Mrs. Goldsmith; (G) Sarah, April 24, 1794-deceasee; married Joseph Mast, of family 3311, note; one of the first four families in Walnutcreek Township, Holmes County, Ohio; (H) Mary, August 2, 1798-___; (I) Moses, 9168.

9164. **Peter P. Miller**, 9163, married Barbara Yoder, daughter of Jacob and Elizabeth Yoder, of family 4135, note. (A) John, married Anna Beachy; *Beachy Genealogy* families 239-50; (B) Jacob, married Magdalena Beachy; *Beachy Genealogy* families 151-55; (C) Mary, wife of Adam Yoder, of family 2992; (D) Sally, wife of Mr. Saylor; (E) Daniel, married Barbara Gnagey, of family

4934; (F) Peter, married Catherine Beachy; *Beachy Genealogy* families 510-16; (G) Joseph, 9165; (H) Catherine, wife of Benjamin Schrock; (I) Samuel P., of Meyersdale, Pennsylvania; (J) Moses, 9166; (K) Susan; (L) Lydia, wife of Ephraim Miller, of Mechanicsburg, Pennsylvania.

9165. **Joseph Miller**, 9164, lived at Sharon Center, Iowa; married Sally Stutzman; Samuel, married Anna Yansey; Barbara, died single; Lucy, married Jonas Miller; Catherine, single; Nancy, married Joel Gingerich.

9166. **Moses Miller**, 9164, lived at Kalona, Iowa; married 1) Lydia Schrock; married 2) Catherine Gingerich; David, married Catherine Yoder; Mahlon, killed in a runaway accident as a boy; Eliza, married Joseph S. Yoder; Barbara, married Daniel Wertz; Mary, married David Swartzendruber; Lydia, died at five years.

9167. **Jonas Miller**, 9163, was born August 11, 1788, and was one of the first four families in Walnutcreek Township, Holmes County, Ohio. He married Catherine Hershberger, of family 4569, note. (A) Moses, January 12, 1811-____, an Amish bishop; married Catherine Dunn, of families 5090, 5412, and 6323; (B) Mary, married Joseph Mast, son of Jacob Mast; see family 517, note; (C) Elizabeth, married Isaac Miller, born March 23, 1811; died January 30, 1892, of *Gnagey Genealogy* family 10; see family 4763; (D) Peter, married Veronica Miller, daughter of John or Annas Miller, *of Gnagey Genealogy* family 19; (E) Catherine, married Peter Miller, son of Isaac Miller, of family 9160; (F) Sally, died single; (G) Jacob, married Anna Schrock, of family 4474; (H) Barbara, married Jacob Stutzman; (I) Dinah, married John Speicher; (J) Susanna, married Peter Beachy, of *Beachy Genealogy* family 138; see families 4581, 5575, 5728, 5739; (K) Elias, married Philipine Reber, and resides, at seventy-eight years, on the old homestead of his father (1911).

9168. **Moses Miller**, 9163, known as "Gross Mose," was born January 28, 1802; married Catherine Miller, daughter of "Broad Run" John Miller, of family 9175. He moved to Ohio in 1820, and was a bishop in the Amish Church; Mary, died single at thirty-five years; Sarah; died single at seventy-five years; Jonathan, married Magdalena Stutzman, of families 5078, 5674, 5747, 5751; John, married Susanna Schrock, of families 2235, 4003, 4008, 4271, 4486; Catherine, married Tobias Kauffman; Moses, married Magdalena Schrock, of families 1683, 4412; Peter, married Barbara Sommers, daughter of Elizabeth Miller and Joseph Sommers, of family 9152.

9169. **Joseph Miller**, 9146, of Conemaugh Township, Somerset County, Pennsylvania, married 1) Miss Gehman; Yost, of Conemaugh Township; Maria, wife of Joseph Hostetler, of family 7336; Elizabeth, wife of Stephen Kauffman. Married 2) Barbara Bontrager; Daniel, 9170; Joseph, 9171; John, 9172; Sarah, wife of Philip Weirich; Frany, wife of Joseph Hershberger.

9170. **Daniel Miller**, 9169, Middlebury, Indiana, was a bishop in the Amish Church; see family 7449.

9171. **Joseph Miller**, 9169, was one of the first settlers in Lagrange County, Indiana. He married Elizabeth Yoder, who was born July 12, 1812; died April 1881; daughter of Joseph Yoder, son of Christian Yoder; of family 3695, note; see family 2931.

9172. **John S. Miller**, 9169, Middlebury, Indiana; married Margaret Sutter; see families 3528 and 3538.
9173. **Catherine Miller**, 9146, of Conemaugh Township, Somerset County, Pennsylvania; married Jacob Kauffman; Solomon, of families 7035-7110; John, of Conemaugh Township; Jacob, of Iowa; Jonas, of Michigan; Moses, an Amish preacher of Indiana; Mrs. John Thomas; Catherine, wife of Daniel Yoder, of family 3065; Mrs. Jacob Garber, of Davidsville, Pennsylvania.
9174. **Mrs. Christian Mishler**, 9146, had children: Tobias; Christian; Jonas; Mrs. David Weaver; Catherine, and Elizabeth, who both died single at an advanced age.

Historic Miller Farms in Ohio

The farm of Moses J. Miller, Klein or Glee Mose Miller, north of Walnut Creek, Ohio. Moses was a leader of an Old Order Amish group in Holmes County, Credit: J. Virgil Miller.

The farm of Gross Mose Miller, leader of the church-building Amish near Walnut Creek. The farm is now owned by James A. Miller, a fifth-generation descendant. Pictured are James and his daughter. Credit: J. Virgil Miller.

APPENDIX NO. II

The Glades Amish of Brothersvalley

A Bicentennial Study First Appeared
In the *Berlin Bicentennial Book* in 1976

by Thomas Irvin Maust II

August 3, 1976

Introduction

Like an intricate jigsaw puzzle, the piecing together of the evidence concerning the Glades Amish of Brothersvalley is a tedious process. The nearly complete absence of written Amish records necessitates reference to legal and governmental documents, traditions, family histories, immigration records, cemeteries, etc. And, considering the traditionally independent and anti-government stance of the Amish, along with the isolation of early Brothersvalley from governmental centers, even the official governmental records are sometimes questionable. Nevertheless, the pieces are now beginning to look like a whole, and the result is surprising—surprising because the Amish, who were so important to the early settlement of our area, have for decades vanished from Brothersvalley.

This study is an attempt to form this scattered evidence into a reasonable history of some of our earliest pioneers—The Glades Amish of Brothersvalley.

Acknowledgements

The works of Paul V. Hostetler and Dr. Hugh Gingerich, as well as the personal library of Catherine J. Miller, have been of invaluable aid in the preparation of this study.

The Glades Amish of Brothersvalley

A persistent failing of local histories by local historians has been the omission of the history of the Amish church and community in what is now Brothersvalley Township in Somerset County, Pennsylvania. Indeed, the very suggestion of such a history may come as a surprise to today's local residents. Nevertheless, it is possible to establish several facts about the Glades Amish and to add some well-grounded speculations.

First, the Amish, along with their German Brethren neighbors,* migrated from eastern Pennsylvania to become the earliest permanent settlers in Brothersvalley. As early as the mid-1720s, trappers and hunters had been bringing buffalo and other hides to eastern Pennsylvania from the wilderness which was then the Brothersvalley glades.[1] And, no doubt, as word of the area's potential was rumored by these frontiersmen and, as the population pressures of the large German families increased, there were those who joined their neighbors and moved from the overcrowded east to the open wilds beyond the Allegheny Mountain. Therefore, it is hardly surprising that most of the old Brothersvalley names can now be traced directly to neighboring homesteads in eastern counties of the state.

So it was that as early as the 1750s[2] and definitely by the 1760s, Amish neighbors down east had migrated through the dense mountain forests and resettled as neighbors again in an area beginning at what is now the town of Berlin, and stretching north along two parallel branches which are the headwaters of the Stony Creek. Many of these early settlers were vanguards of civilization who preceded even the surveyors and tax collectors into the Brothersvalley wilderness and whose tomahawk claims defied the Proclamation Line of 1763.** At this early date, these pioneers' primary concern was survival rather than the legalities of an English-speaking government.

Among the early Amish settlers here were John Schrock (Schrack, Schrag, Schryack, Shrake) and Christian Blough (Blauch, Plough). A Schrock family sketch tells us that John, as a young boy, came with his half-brother to the vicinity of Berlin in or about 1765.[3] Although the sketch calls him a Mennonite, he was certainly Amish, and later on married one of his Amish neighbors, a sister of Amish Bishop Jacob Miller (see below). Schrock grew to manhood here, purchased land from the Speichers (also below), died in 1813, and lies buried on

---

H. Austin Cooper's Two Centuries of Brothersvalley Church of the Brethren *deals with this history. However, although his overall history is generally accurate, Cooper erred greatly in listing many of the early Amish as Brethren and Lutheran. Appendix 1 of this study lists the Amish who were plotted on the first warrant map of Brothersvalley or who were listed in the first tax assessment for Brothersvalley.*

**The proclamation officially prohibited settlement west of the Allegheny Mountains and remained in effect until 1768.*

---

[1] Sanford G. Shetler, *Two Centuries of Struggle and Growth* (Scottdale, Pa.: 1963), p. 14.
[2] *Ibid.*, p. 15
[3] William H. Welfley, *History of Bedford and Somerset Counties, Pennsylvania* (New York: 1906), III, p. 62.

the Lewis Maust farm. Christian Blough settled in 1767[4] on what is now the William Shultz farm, an area which, according to one Mennonite historian, became a sizable Amish settlement.[5] He died at the early age of thirty-three and was buried there in 1777. These graves remain today.

Apparently during the late 1760s, a heavy migration of Amish came to the glades, mostly from Berks County, Pennsylvania. Much of the land which is today immediately north of Berlin was held at one time or another by these Amish. There is strong evidence that these Brothersvalley pioneers were actively supported by the Amish Church in eastern Pennsylvania. An old *Amish Alms Book*, containing financial records from 1768 onward for the Amish of the Reading-Berks County area, in a section kept by Deacon Hans Kurtz, lists a gift on November 15, 1768, of "XI pounds and six Pence"* to Christian Spelcher,[6] who shortly thereafter came to Brothersvalley from Berks County and settled where Mr. And Mrs. Lewis Maust now live. Since that sum was nearly the whole amount contained in the treasury at that time, it would seem virtually certain to have been a major contribution from the eastern Amish Church to the pioneer Amish community struggling to survive in the Brothersvalley glades.

Certainly the most well-known Amishman to settle here in those early years was young Joseph Schantz (anglicized to Johns or Johnes) who came to America in 1769 at age twenty and settled soon thereafter with the Amish in Brothersvalley.[7] Part of his claim was in the heart of what is now Berlin, and it is difficult for us to imagine the dense, virgin wilderness he found there. Jacob Keffer's original indenture for the town of Berlin on Plus Spring lists "Joseph Johnes" as an owner of an adjoining tract. And, the first addition to Berlin, that part west from Division Street and including the upper diamond, was purchased by Jacob Keffer, John Fisher, and Francis Hay from Amishman Joseph Johnes. The agreement was made in 1787, but like so many early land transactions, was not deeded until 1796.[8] Joseph Johns finally sold all of his Brothersvalley property in 1793[9] and relocated at the confluence of the Conemaugh River where he founded a city which today bears his name—Johnstown, Pennsylvania.

Another notable Amish leader came to the Brothersvalley glades with the migration from eastern Pennsylvania. He was Jacob Miller, the first leader of the River Amish in Elk Lick (the church and community there remain active

---

* *The original German text reads:* "mer in disen iahr aus geben von dem arm geld au Christ Schpicher XI fund und sechs benz." *Miller's translation reads:* "more paid out in this year of the alms money to Christ Speicher 11 pounds and six pence."

---

[4] Elias Gnagey, *A Complete History of Christian Gnaegi* (Elkhart, Ind.: 1897), p. 136.
[5] Shetler, p. 51.
[6] *Amish Alms Book (1768)*, translated by Catherine J. Miller (original copy from her library).
[7] *Annals of the Conestoga Valley*, p. 247.
[8] Welfley, II, p. 589.
[9] Mast, p. 247.

today).[10] Jacob was a son of Hannes Miller, Sr., (known as "Indian John"*) who was an early Amish settler on what is now the Tom Maust farm. About 1782 at age twenty-eight, Jacob and his young family moved to the glades where his father had settled a few years before.[11] While there he ministered to the Brothersvalley Amish before moving to Elk Lick sometime between 1785 and 1793, and finally moving again to Tuscarawas County, Ohio, where he became the first Amish Mennonite leader before his death in 1835.[12] His mother, Magdalena, is buried on the home farm in Brothersvalley. The old cemetery is on an elevated ridge and looks west across the whole valley, which was once the core of the Amish community. The hand-chiseled stone reads "M1817M." One of Jacob's brothers, known as Glades Christian to distinguish him from nearly half a dozen local Christian Millers, remained on the home farm and became a prominent Brothersvalley farmer in the early 1800s.[13] The Miller sisters became Mrs. Joseph Speicher, Mrs. Christian Speicher, Mrs. Christian Mishler, Mrs. John Schrock, and Mrs. Jacob Kauffman. We can easily see from these family names that the Amish family of Hannes Miller, Sr., in keeping with Amish tradition, married members of other neighboring Amish families.[14]

Christian Zug (Zook), although not famous to our generation, must certainly have been famous to his generation in Brothersvalley, for not only did he settle where Mr. and Mrs. Jim Will now live sometime about or before 1770, but shortly thereafter six of his sons, sons-in-law, and stepsons-in-law settled on nearby farms.[15] Such family ties, as we have already seen, were as common then as they are today among the Amish.

(A detailed list of the earliest Amish settlers in Brothersvalley begins on page 112.)

Second, the Amish Church in the Brothersvalley glades just north of Berlin was active for approximately the next 125 years.[16] Amish-Mennonite records tell us that Bishop Jacob Mast (Maust), born in 1738 and died 1808, was a Berks County Amish leader of considerable ability who was charged with all of the Amish settlements in Pennsylvania, including three west of the Susquehanna River, one of which was the Glades.[17] More evidence of the Brothersvalley Amish comes from a conference of Somerset County Amish ministers held in 1837. At that meeting, these six men signed the final document as ministers to the Glades Church: Christian Yoder, Sr. (Son of Schweitzer Yoder); Christian

---

The story of "Indian John" Miller is told on pages 33 and 953 of Descendants of Jacob Hochstetler.

---

[10] Shetler, p. 332.
[11] *Joel B. Miller History*, p. 15.
[12] Virgil Miller, *Descendants of Daniel B. Miller* (1970), p. 2.
[13] Welfley, II, p. 585.
[14] *DJH*, p. 339.
[15] Paul V. Hostetler, notes on the Amish in Lebanon and then Somerset Cos., Dec. 22, 1973.
[16] Shetler, p. 322.
[17] *Ibid.*, p. 319.

Yoder, Jr.,* Abraham Miller; Jacob Miller (not the same as above); Jacob Schwartzendruber; and David Yoder.[18] The text of the document, entitled *The Discipline of 1837*, is found in Apprendix II.

A Mennonite historian suggests that by the early 1800s, these Amish on the Stony Creek numbered up to 100 members in possibly three congregations.[19] On October 3, 1830, these churches hosted at least one of the church-wide Amish conferences.[20] Another sign of vigor during the first thirty-five years of the 1800s was the continuing migration of Amish from the mother country into the community. Among these later Amish immigrants were Daniel Brenneman and his wife, Mary Bender Brenneman, who brought their family from Germany in 1825[21] and lived temporarily in David Lehman's house near Berlin, where their last daughter, Barbara, was born on April 5, 1827.[22] they farmed in Brothersvalley briefly as tenants before moving to the Elk Lick area.[23] Also, the aforementioned Jacob Schwartzendruber, one of the signers of *The Discipline of 1837*, was ordained as an Amish minister in Mengeringhausen, Waldeck, Germany, in 1826 before coming to America in 1833. He, too, settled first in Brothersvalley and ministered to the church there until 1840, when he joined in the movement south to Elk Lick.[24]

And yet, in spite of these signs of strength, by 1850 the local church had reached its zenith and mysteriously was nonexistent by the early years of the new century. The last bishop, Abner Yoder (grandson of Christian, Jr.), migrated west to Johnson County, Iowa, in 1866,[25] and, according to *The Mennonite Encyclopedia*, the last services were probably held during the 1870s. The same source reports that "Jacob B. Schrock, a jurist of Berlin, Pa., recalled in a personal interview in 1950, that as a boy he accompanied his parents on a visit to his grandparents, the Michael Schrocks, about 1879, and saw the old benches stacked on the back porch, left there after the last preaching service of the Amish in that community."[26]

The History of Bedford and Somerset Counties, published in 1906, mentions a sprinkling of Amish still living then in Brothersvalley and Stony

---

* Dr. E. C. Saylor and J. B. Schrock in 1946 wrote a brief summary of the Yoder Cemeteries in Stonycreek Township. One of these "...contains the graves of four adults said to be Yoders whose descendants now live near Haven and Yoder, Kansas. Christian Yoder Senior and Junior both Amish ministers."

---

[18] Harold S. Bender, "Some Early American Amish Mennonite Disciplines," *The Mennonite Quarterly Review*, VII (Apr. 1934), pp. 93-95.
[19] Shetler, p. 324.
[20] "Somerset County," *The Mennonite Encyclopedia* (1959), IV, p. 574.
[21] Albert H. Gerberich, *The Brenneman History* (Scottdale, Pa.: 1938), p. 856
[22] Brenneman Family Bible, transcript by Catherine J. Miller.
[23] Gerberich, p. 857.
[24] "Somerset County," *The Mennonite Encyclopedia*, p. 574.
[25] Shetler, p. 324.
[26] "Somerset County," *The Mennonite Encyclopedia*, p. 574.

Creek Townships.²⁷ However, in 1910 the last local member on record died at the age of ninety-three.²⁸ He was Benedict Yoder.

And so we ask the obvious: What was the fate of this once prosperous Amish settlement? To answer, we offer three reasons. First,. migrations west to the lure of cheap and more fertile land, and north, like Joseph Johns, and south, like Jacob Swartzendruber, to the growing Amish settlements in Conemaugh and Elk Like definitely was an early factor in weakening the Brothersvalley Amish. Indeed, common local Amish names of the 1760-1840 period, such as Schantz (Johns), Mishler, Dieffenbaugh, Troyer (Dreyer), Zug (Zook), Schwartzendruber, and Brenneman, completely vanished from the township in subsequent years ass whole families migrated north, south, and west. One such exodus occurred in 1812 when the Jacob Zug family moved to Holmes County, Ohio.²⁹ Jacob was the son of the aforementioned Christian, and several of that family are buried on Christian's home farm in Brothersvalley.

Second, internal dispute and division concerning moral behavior and adoption of modern lifestyles was a further factor in the decline of the Brothersvalley Amish. The contents of *The Discipline of 1837* (see Appendix II) are abundant evidence of both widespread immorality and adoption of worldly customs. Later, as the Civil War raged, Amish ministers condemned Amish youth for their immoral behavior while others were dying on the battlefields.³⁰ Part of the immorality problem was the bizarre custom of "bundling, " in which the prospective Amish bride and groom slept in the same bed, but were fully clothed and separated by a plank.³¹ Besides condemning this immorality, the signers of *The Discipline of 1837* came down hard against loud colors, high collars, silk neckerchiefs, and mirrors in the house. These controversies apparently became so widespread and so weakened the Glades Amish of Brothersvalley that, in the words of their contemporaries, "The people became too ungodly and the church could not stand."³²

Weakened internally, then, by migrations and by strife, we are logically led to a third fate of the Brothersvalley Amish. Since they and the Brethren had coexisted for generations as neighbors in the Berlin-Brotherton-Roxbury triangle of Brothersvalley Township (and nearby portions of what is now Stony Creek Township), our third possibility is that the strong and evangelistic Brethren simply absorbed many of the Amish. Brethren histories tell us of many intense evangelistic efforts sponsored by that denomination, especially during the so-called "Second Awakening" of 1785-1800.³³ also, the practices of the Amish and Brethren were similar in an age when horses and buggies, lanterns, and homemade plain clothes were normal. Creek baptism, which was standard among the Brethren (hence the name Tunker or Dunkard), was not unusual among some Amish

---

[27] Welfley, II, p. 502.
[28] Shetler, p. 324.
[29] Paul V. Hostetler, unpublished letter, Nov. 18, 1974.
[30] Shetler, p. 324.
[31] *Ibid.,* p. 45.
[32] "Somerset County, *The Mennonite Encyclopedia*, p. 574.
[33] H. Austin Cooper, *Two Centuries of Brothersvalley Church of the Brethren* (1962), p. 218.

circles.[34] Indeed, what minor doctrinal differences did exist between the groups were easily breached by the German language which was, of course, native to both. Combining these factors, then, with the probable internal weakness of the Amish, the case becomes even stronger. Many descendants of the early Amish pioneers later joined the Brethren, the United Brethren, or other denominations. Among these were the local descendants of Christian Blough (although those descendants who migrated north remained active for some time in Amish-Mennonite circles) and the John Schrock family (a son joined the Disciples of Christ).[35] Even today, many local families bear names which are historically Amish.

In addition to the many local family names, traces of the Old Amish Lane, which ran through the heart of the early settlement, remain today as a vague legacy to the Amish of Brothersvalley. On the banks of the Stony Creek at the northern line of the Berlin Community Grove can be seen the approach embankments to an old bridge which carried the lane across the creek. Several decades ago the bridge was barricaded and soon after was washed away in a storm. The WPA Cemetery Survey for Brothersvalley Township describes the Lehman Cemetery on the Webreck farm as being located "...on the north side of an abandoned road, known as the Amish Lane...." The cemetery and remains of the lane are still seen. Indeed, many older residents of the area recall crossing the valley between Berlin and Route 31 on east-west lanes in their younger days, but the name Amish Lane apparently originated generations before even the oldest living residents. Traces of an east-west lane are seen in the *1876 County Atlas of Somerset,*[36] but none on that map run the whole breadth of the area. Thus, more than a century ago, the Amish Lane meandered among Amish farms in a general east-west direction, connecting the forerunners of what we now know as the Webreck Road, the Beulah Road, and the Roxbury Road. Its traces today, scattered through the heartland and oral history of Brothersvalley, survive as one of the few reminders of Brothersvalley's enigmatic Amish community.

---

[34] Shetler, p. 329.
[35] Welfley, III, p. 62.
[36] F. W. Beers, *County Atlas of Somerset, Pennsylvania*, (New York: F.W. Beers and Co., 1876) p. 61.

A Map of the Glades Amish of Brothersvalley
1767-1785

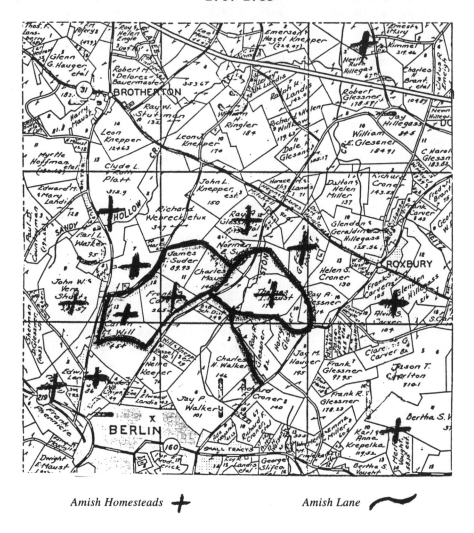

Amish Homesteads ✢   Amish Lane ⌇

EARLIEST BROTHERSVALLEY WARRANT MAP: The following names plotted on the first Brothersvalley Warrant Map were Amish. Parenthetical information describes the approximate locations of these plots as found in the *1972 Somerset County Plat Book*.

Berkey, Jacob - warrant date unknown
   (Frank S. Carver tract adjoining Calvin M. Will. Berkey possibly was not Amish.)

Blough, Christian - 1773 warrant
(Southern part of Sherman D. Glessner, Jr., and John W. and Vera Shultz tracts)
Diefenbach, Casper - 1785 warrant
(Deeter's Gap)
Johns, Joseph - 1785 warrant
(Frank Phennicle and upper diamond area of Berlin)
Leman/Lehman, Benedict - 1773 warrant
(Alvin S. Carver, southern part of Glenden A. Hillegass, eastern part of Clarence G. Carver, and Jason T. Charlton)
Leman(Lehman), John - 1785 warrant
(Karl and Anna Krepelka, Merl Vought, est., and western part of Bertha S. Vought)
Miller, Nicholas - 1773 warrant
(Norman E. Suder and Ray A. Glessner, et al.)
Mishler, Joseph - warrant date unknown
(Northern part of John W. and Vera Shultz, Earl L. Walker, and Southern tip of Clyde L. and Ruth Platt)
Schrock, Casper - 1773 warrant
(Southeastern part of Calvin M. Will and Nellie Keefer)
Speicher, Christian - 1809 warrant
(Fern Glessner Maust)
Yoder, Christian - 1773 warrant
(Stony Creek Township)
Yoder, David - 1777 warrant
(Stony Creek Township)
Zug, Christian - 1773 warrant
(James I. Suder)
Zug, John - 1773 warrant
(Edwin P. Landis, Snyder's Potato Chips, Inc., Elwood Landis, part of Berlin Borough)

OTHER EARLY AMISH: The following names occur on early Brothersvalley tax assessments, deeds, or warrants.

Blough (miscopied Benuch, Christopher) Christian - 1773 tax
Johns, Joseph - 1775 tax
Lehman, Peter - 1779 tax
Miller, Hannes, Sr. - 1785 warrant
Schrock, Jacob - 1779 tax
Spiker, Christian - 1773 tax
Troyer, John - 1775 tax
Troyer, Michael - 1775 tax
Yoder, John - 1775 deed

The Discipline of 1837
River, Glade, Conemaugh Congregations, Pennsylvania, March 18, 1837

Concerning the Conference of the Ministry of the Three Congregations, River, Glade, and Conemaugh. Decisions as follows:

First: It is noted that decline has set in because the ordinance of God in the matter of the ban is greatly neglected. Decided that separation and shunning are to be practiced toward all disobedient ones without regard of person, whether man or woman.

Second: It is noted that there is awful pride in clothing, namely with respect to silken neck cloths (*Halstuecher*) worn around the neck, so that mothers tie silken neckcloths on their children, and make high collars on their children's shirts and clothing; and the mothers permit their daughters to wear men's hats and go with them to church or other places, or that even the mothers have them themselves. Decided that such things shall not be among us.

Third: Decided that there shall be no display in houses, namely where houses are built or painted with various colors, or filled with showy furniture, namely with wooden, porcelain, or glass utensils (dishes), and having cupboards and mirrors hung on the wall and such things.

Fourth: Decided that worldly offices are not to be held, namely serving on juries, or holding elections to elect officials.

Fifth: Decided that excessive driving of sleighs or other vehicles is not to be, and also that vehicles are not to be painted with two colors, as has already occurred too much.

Sixth: Decided that those who marry outside are no longer to be received again so lightly into fellowship, unless they bring their marriage partners with them into Christian discipline, and are received after true repentance and change of heart has been shown.

Seventh: Decided that when two persons marry, both of whom are outside the church, and they desire to be received into fellowship, the ministers shall make plain to them the obligations of Christian marriage according to the ordinance of God, and when they are received they shall promise before God and the brotherhood to fulfill the obligations of Christian marriage according to Christian ordinance.

Eighth: Decided that the Sabbath is to be kept holy, that business is to be conducted on the six days of the week according to the ordinance, and Sunday is to be kept to the honor of God, except in case of emergency.

Ninth: With regard to the excesses practiced among the youth, namely that the youth take the liberty to sleep or lie together without any fear or shame, such things shall not be tolerated at all. And when it takes place with the knowledge of the parents and something bad happens on account of it, the parents shall not go unpunished.

Tenth: Decided that the tailors are not to make new or worldly styles of clothing for members of the church, but are to follow the old style and such as is indicated by the ministers and older people of the church.

Eleventh: Likewise, the cabinetmakers are not to make such proud kinds of furniture and not decorate them with such loud or gay (*scheckich*) colors.

Twelfth: In conclusion, all the above-mentioned articles are to be observed according to the Christian discipline and practice.

Signed by us, ministers of the three above-named congregations.

>   Conemaugh Congregation
>   Jacob Oesch
>   Christian Miller
>   Christian Nissli
>   Joseph Miller
>   Jonas Yoder
>
>   Glade Congregation
>   Christian Yoder, Senior
>   Christian Yoder, Junior
>   Abraham Miller
>   Jacob Swartzendruber
>   David Yoder
>
>   River Congregation
>   Benedict Miller
>   Jost Yoder
>   Hannes Gingrich

Translated and edited by Harold S. Bender, "Some Early American Amish Mennonite Disciplines," *The Mennonite Quarterly Review* (Apr. 1934), Vol. 8, No. 2, pp. 93-95.

Appendix No. III

A Trip to the Glades
Reflections on the Homestead–June 18, 1996

by J. Virgil Miller

After spending an unpleasantly rainy evening in Somerset, squeezed in a little economy motel, I awoke refreshed; outside there was fog and drizzle, but very fresh air. The papers predicted more rain, and we got it from time to time. I treated myself to a breakfast of McDonald's pancakes, sausage, and coffee. This was the McDonald's just off the turnpike, but the breakfast clientele was the same as in Sarasota—a gathering of seniors reading the paper, sipping refills of senior coffee, and chewing the rag, exchanging views about what was wrong with the world. One man answered my statement that when I was in high school, hamburgers and coffee were a nickel apiece by saying that in spite of that, things are better now.

But I was going to dig much farther into the past. My Miller ancestor, John or Hannes Miller, came to America in 1749 and had his final resting place near Berlin, Pennsylvania, in Somerset County, about ten miles away. I had been there before, so it was no longer a voyage of discovery. I know the man who lives there and I know how to get there. I stopped briefly at Brotherton, a village on the highway between Somerset and Bedford, the capital of the colonial territory at the time of Braddock's defeat—then British. John Miller came to Bedford County just before the Revolution, and just after the French and Indian War, when it was safe to come west of the Appalachians. Somerset County was part of Bedford until 1795, so for any early records, one has to look in Bedford. I had done that the day before in the nicely preserved colonial town of Bedford at a modest courthouse still being used, with a steeple like a church.

Here I was, pausing at Brotherton, half way between Somerset and Bedford. The region is called the Glades, a valley sweeping north of the highway, in wonderful alternation of wooded hills and mountains in the back; to the north, the township is called Stony Creek, which is a stream starting at Berlin in the south and flowing through the whole valley to the north. To the south is Brothers Valley, named for the Brethren who were prominent missionaries in early days, and whose presence is shown by their churches dotted over the valley and the nearby towns. I paused at the Brethren Cemetery at Brotherton. I was looking for traces of Amish who left the valley more than a century ago. Those who left migrated further west to Ohio, Indiana, and further. Those who stayed joined the Brethren. My ancestors were Amish, and I saw familiar names: Miller, Schrock, Yoder, and Blough, all Amish names.

The owner of the original Miller farm is Tom Maust, also recognizable as an Amish name, though the family belongs to the Church of Christ. Tom has a deed with John Miller's name on it, calling the farm Miller's Choice. I know him quite well after a half-dozen previous visits. His wife welcomed me with a bowl of soup and some coffee. The house is modern and comfortable, looking like any other substantial farm home with wooden siding painted white, but underneath are logs eight to ten inches thick. Tom showed me a portion of a log that he had cut out the previous year in order to make an additional room.

We talked about our families—the wives are more interested in their immediate families than in the original settlers. Tom was telling me how he is beginning to enjoy showing bus loads of people who come to see the Miller farm, many of them still Amish, from Ohio, Indiana, and other states. There still are Old Order Amish living in the extreme south of the county. I expressed a wish to see the "Amish Lane," an old road used by the early settlers to go between their farms back in the late 1700s and early 1800s. Interestingly, the person who most ardently pursued the history of the Amish community was Tom's son, Tom, Jr., who was originally going to settle in the Glades on the heritage farm. But the Mausts had been hosting exchange students from Europe, a girl from Germany and a young man from Norway for periods of time. Tom, Jr., and the Norwegian youth got along so well that on an exchange visit to Norway, Tom met his friend's female cousin, and after getting better acquainted, eventually married her. He wanted to bring her to the States and settle in the Glades, but after a few years his wife got homesick for Norway. And so they compromised—he is working in Norway for an American company, and they come home for a month every year. By now they have three handsome European-type children who are almost in high school. I first met Tom, Jr., when he was a college student about twenty years ago on a visit with my genealogist friend, Paul Hostetler. Tom wrote a fine article about the Amish community for the *Berlin Centennial* some years ago.

Meanwhile, Tom, Sr., has developed an interest in his heritage. The Maust name was originally Mast and is a well-known Amish or Mennonite name. Tom said one can see the Amish Lane better from his brother's farm. From there we could see the line of the Amish Lane that led to the farms of Casper Schrag, Nicholas Miller, Christian Speicher, and Benedict Lehman. Tom was one of the children of his father, and he and his brothers each received a farm, but his youngest brother, Charles, got the home place.

We stopped at the Calvin Will farm to see the cemetery where Casper Schrag is buried. His nephew, John Schrock, lived nearby and was married to John Miller's daughter. Other Miller children who lived in the area were the wives of two sons of Christian Speicher, John Miller's neighbor to the north. Christian Speicher, Jr., lived on his father's farm, and Joseph Speicher lived a few miles north in Stony Creek Township. Nicholas Miller was John Miller's brother. Though he took out a warrant for the farm northwest of the John Miller homestead, he never came to Somerset County, but likely his son Christian did. Benedict Lehman, who we have some reason to believe was John

Mr. & Mrs. Thomas Maust, Sr., at their home near Berlin, Pennsylvania, have a deed showing John Miller, Sr., transferring the farm "Miller's Choice" to his son Christian in 1785.

Mr. Maust standing in "Amish Lane," still called that by local residents. It was a narrow lane leading to the various Amish farms. See article by Thomas Maust II. Photos by J. Virgil Miller.

Miller's brother-in-law, lived a bit east of the Maust farm. On the Maust farm itself is a small cemetery with several markers, only one of which has an inscription. It reads: "M1817M," which we could interpret as: Magdalena Miller, died 1817. The 1798 estate settlement of John Miller is one of the earliest in the Somerset County Courthouse. So this is indeed a historic farm. Mr. Maust and I followed the Amish Lane for a bit; it was grown over like some forgotten Roman road in England or Turkey, but only wide enough for a buggy or farm wagon. I took a few pictures and realized that this was a historic community from the past with only a few markers to show that my ancestors once lived there.

Index

— A —

Alleshouse, Margaret, 32
Amman, Jacob, 23
Amman, Jakob, 23
Arnold family, 29, 30
Arnold, George, 30
Ashe, Catherine, 98

— B —

Bale, Catherine, 98
Beachey, Elizabeth, 36
Beachey, Moses, 36
Beachy, Abraham, 101
Beachy, Anna, 101
Beachy, Catherine, 43, 97, 101, 102
Beachy, Elizabeth, 101
Beachy, Leroy, 41
Beachy, Magdalena, 101
Beachy, Moses, 99
Beachy, Peter, 43, 102
Beachy, Sarah, 36
Beachy, Susanna, 102
Beegley, Michael, 6
Beiler, 2
Bender, Catherine, 97
Bender, Mary, 98
Bender, William, 97
Benuch, Christopher, 113
Berkey, 2
Berkey, Barbara, 55
Berkey, David, 54, 55
Berkey, Jacob, 112
Berkey, Samuel, 67
Berkey, Susanna, 80
Berkey, Widow, 54
Biddle, Jacob, 97
Biddle, Mary, 97
Bierden, George, 59
Bitsche, Catherine, 43
Bitsche, Peter, 43, 97
Bitsche, Sally, 97
Bitschi, Moses, 61
Bittinger family, 30
Blauch, Christian, 106
Blauman, Sally, 97
Blough family, 2, 69
Blough, Anna, 66
Blough, Christ, 107
Blough, Christian, 7, 57, 58, 66, 106, 111, 113
Blough, David, 80, 85
Blough, Elizabeth, 66, 67, 85
Blough, Fanny, 71
Blough, Freny, 57, 61, 66
Blough, Henry, 66, 67
Blough, Jacob, 66, 74
Blough, John, 71
Blough, Joseph, 66
Blough, Magdalena, 74, 80
Blough, Mary, 85
Blough, Peter, 59
Bluebaugh family, 30
Bontrager, Andrew, 45, 46, 67
Bontrager, Barbara, 65, 67, 102
Bontrager, Christian, 67, 68
Bontrager, John, 67, 101
Bontrager, Magdalena, 101
Bontrager, Martin, 67
Bornträger, Johann Martin, 89
Bornträger, Martin, 90
Borntreger, Barbara, 68
Borntreger, Christian, 68, 99
Borntreger, David, 68
Borntreger, Elizabeth, 68
Borntreger, Hansi, 68
Borntreger, John E., 68
Borntreger, Joseph, 68
Borntreger, Lydia, 68
Borntreger, Maria, 68
Borntreger, Susanna, 99
Bowman, Bill, 46
Bowman, William, Mr./Mrs., 47
Brenneman, 110
Brenneman, Anna, 98
Brenneman, Barbara, 109
Brenneman, Catherine, 97
Brenneman, Christian, 48, 49
Brenneman, Daniel, 109
Brenneman, Elizabeth, 101
Brenneman, Jacob, 98
Brenneman, Mary, 48, 49
Brenneman, Mary Bender, 109
Buchele, Michael, 6
Burcky, 27
Bürcky, Christian, 89

— C —

Carvel, Catherine, 98
Carvel, Elias, 98
Carver, Alvin S., 113
Carver, Clarence G., 113
Carver, Frank S., 112
Charlton, Jason T., 113
Christner, 4
Christner, Hans, 70
Cober, Magdalena, 75
Cophet, Frene, 24
Correll, Mrs., 97
Coxson, Abraham, 4, 6, 7

— D —

Danner, Peter, 25
Davis, Sam, 40, 43
Degler, Catherine, 99
Dellenbach, Peter, 59
Detweiler, Melchior, 1, 14
Diefenbach, Casper, 113
Dieffenbaugh, 110
Drachsel, Abraham, 74
Dreyer, 110
Drumm, Ernst, 25
Dunn, Catherine, 102

— E —

Eash, Anna, 66
Eash, Barbara, 68, 80
Eash, Catherine, 49
Eash, Daniel, 59
Eash, Elizabeth, 97
Eash, Henry, 66
Eash, Isaac, 97
Eash, Jonathan, 66
Eash, Lydia, 80
Eash, Magdalena, 80
Eash, Sem K., 52
Egli, Nicolaus, 24
Ehrich, Catherine, 97
Esch, Johannes, 89

— F —

Fike, 29
Fike, Barbara, 71
Fike, Samuel R., 47
Fisher, 2
Fisher, John, 107
Follmer, Marie, 35, 38
Folmer, Maria, 99
Forney, Joseph, 82
Frey, Elsbeth, 24
Frey, Polly, 101

— G —

Garber, Jacob, Mrs. 103
Garver, Elizabeth, 55
Garver, John, 55
Garver, Mary, 100
Geeting, John, 34, 37
Gehman, Miss, 102
Gerber, 62

Gerber, Barbara, 62
Gerber, David, 98
Gerber, Johannes, 16
Gerber, Veronica, 100
Gerber, William, 62
Gindelsberger, Catherine, 59, 62
Gindelsberger, Christian, 59, 62
Gindelsberger, Judith, 55
Gindelsberger, Magdalena, 62
Gindelsberger, Margaret, 75
Gindelsperger, Catherine, 98
Gindelsperger, Judith, 98
Gingerich, Catherine, 98, 102
Gingerich, Daniel, 98
Gingerich, Hugh, vii
Gingerich, Hugh, Dr., 105
Gingerich, Joel, 102
Gingerich, Nancy, 102
Gingrich, Hannes, 115
Glessner, Ray A., 113
Glessner, Sherman D., Jr., 113
Gnaegi, Anna, 98
Gnaegi, Christian, 3, 74
Gnaegi, Freny, 86
Gnaegi, Johannes, 16, 86, 90
Gnaegi, Magdalena, 74
Gnaegi, Veronica, 86
Gnagey, 29
Gnagey, Anna, 36, 42
Gnagey, Barbara, 101
Gnagey, Christian, 34, 42
Gnagey, Daniel, 47
Gnagey, Johannes, 34
Gnägi, Christen, 24
Gnägi, Hans, 24
Goldsmith, Mrs., 101
Gorden, Joseph, Mrs., 97
Grabill, Christian, 98
Grabill, Susannah, 98
Guengerich, Barbara, 97
Guengerich, D. P., 97
Guengerich, Jacob, 97
Guengerich, Susanna, 97
Güngerich, 27
Güngerich, Valentine, 26
Güngrich, Velten, 26
Guth, Hermann, vii

— H —

Haage, Barbara, 99
Hay, Francis, 107
Herr, Christian, 5, 6, 7, 18, 20, 22
Hershberger, 2
Hershberger, Anna, 53
Hershberger, Barbara, 99
Hershberger, Catherine, 45, 49, 96, 102
Hershberger, Christian, 101
Hershberger, Daniel, 53
Hershberger, Elizabeth, 101
Hershberger, Frany, 102
Hershberger, Freny, 54, 68
Hershberger, John, 3, 98
Hershberger, Joseph, 68, 102
Hershberger, Leah, 100
Hershberger, Magdalena, 98
Hershberger, Mary, 100, 101
Hershberger, Peter P., 101
Hershberger, Sarah, 97
Hershberger, Veronica, 100
Hertzler, Catherine, 33
Hertzler, Isaac, 100
Hertzler, Jacob, 35
Hertzler, Jacob, Bish., 33
Hertzler, Sarah, 100
Hillegass, Glenden A., 113
Hinckle, Elizabeth, 30, 32
Hochstättler, Erwin, vii
Hochstättler, Isaak, 27
Hochstättler, Jacob, 27
Hochstetler, 4
Hochstetler, Barbara, 4, 5, 6, 8, 9, 19, 28, 29, 30, 31, 32, 33, 46, 96, 98
Hochstetler, Benjamin, 35, 98
Hochstetler, Catherine, 30, 31, 32, 33, 35, 42, 97, 98
Hochstetler, Christian, 6
Hochstetler, E. K., 31
Hochstetler, Edwin Klingaman, 30, 32
Hochstetler, Elizabeth, 30, 32, 99, 100, 101
Hochstetler, Eva, 98
Hochstetler, Freny, 34
Hochstetler, Isaac, 98
Hochstetler, Jacob, 4, 5, 6, 8, 9, 19, 27, 28, 29, 30, 31, 32, 33, 35, 46, 90, 96
Hochstetler, Jacob, Jr., 30
Hochstetler, John, 4, 5, 6, 8, 29, 30, 32, 33, 34, 42, 99
Hochstetler, Jonas, 100
Hochstetler, Joseph, 99
Hochstetler, Lame John, 30
Hochstetler, Lydia, 31
Hochstetler, Margaret, 32
Hochstetler, Mary, 30, 32
Hochstetler, Mollie, 31
Hochstetler, Moses, 98
Hochstetler, Nancy, 99
Hochstetler, Peter, 30, 32
Hochstetler, Samuel, 30, 31, 99
Hochstetler, William F., 1, 19, 96
Hochstettler, Isaak, 89
Holderman, Jacob, 98
Holderman, Rebecca, 98
Holli, Anna, 26
Holli, Barbara, 26
Holli, Christian, 26
Holli, Jakob, 26
Holly, 2, 27
Holly, Barbara, 34
Holly, Christian, 26, 89
Holly, Daniel, 25
Holly, David, 27
Holly, Jacob, 25
Holly, Jakob, 89
Hooley, Veronica, 98
Horner, Margaret, 32
Hostetler, ___, Mrs., 47
Hostetler, Barbara, 67
Hostetler, Gertrude, 98
Hostetler, Jacob, 96, 99
Hostetler, Joseph, 66, 102
Hostetler, Magdalena, 55
Hostetler, Maria, 102
Hostetler, Mary, 66
Hostetler, Paul, ix, 117
Hostetler, Paul V., 20, 22, 105
Hostetler, Peter, 85
Hostetler, Rebecca, 99
Hostetler, Sarah, 85
Hürzeler, Hans, 89

— J —

Jaggi, Johannes, 62
Joder, 27
Joder, Johannes, 89
Joder, Jost, 89
Johnes, Joseph, 107
Johns, 110
Johns, Joseph, 107, 110, 113
Jotter, Christian, 90

— K —

Kauffman, Abraham, 55
Kauffman, Anna, 53
Kauffman, Barbara, 55
Kauffman, Benjamin, 66
Kauffman, Catherine, 7, 51, 52, 53, 54, 56, 69, 80, 91, 102, 103
Kauffman, Christian, 54, 56
Kauffman, Elizabeth, 55, 100, 102
Kauffman, Frene, 24
Kauffman, Freny, 54, 55, 56
Kauffman, Gertrude, 55
Kauffman, Isaac, 62
Kauffman, J., 51

Kauffman, Jacob, vii, 7, 14, 51, 52, 53, 54, 55, 56, 80, 91, 100, 103
Kauffman, Jacob, Mrs., 96, 108
Kauffman, John, 53, 54
Kauffman, John Jacob, 11
Kauffman, Jonas, 52, 53, 56
Kauffman, Lydia, 56
Kauffman, Magdalena, 55, 56, 66, 99
Kauffman, Maria, 53, 55
Kauffman, Mary, 53, 62
Kauffman, Moses, 53, 54, 56
Kauffman, Rebecca, 55, 56
Kauffman, Solomon, 54, 55
Kauffman, Stephen, 66, 102
Kauffman, Susanna, 55
Kauffman, Tobias, 102
Keck, Sarah, 101
Keck, Simon, 101
Keck, Susanna, 55
Keefer, Nellie, 113
Keffer, Jacob, 107
Keim, Catherine, 98
Keim, Catherine Eash, 43
Keim, Freny, 56
Keim, Joseph, 100
Keim, Nicholas, 43, 49
Kempf, John, 97
Kempf, Saloma, 97
Kimmel, Mary, 62
King Louis XIV, 25
Kinsinger family, 36
Klingaman family, 29, 30
Klingaman, Barbara, 71
Klingaman, Catherine, 30, 31, 32
Klingaman, George, 30, 31, 32
Klingaman, John, 71
Klingaman, Lydia, 31
Klingaman, Susanna, 48
Knagey, Christian, 87
Knege, Christian, 3
Knegi, Christian, 24
Knegi, Frene, 24
Knegi, Johannes, 89, 90
Knepp, John, 98
Knepp, Mary, 98
Kreider, Adam, 98
Kreider, Judith, 98
Kreider, Rachel, vii
Krepelka, Anna, 113
Krepelka, Karl, 113
Krider, Katherine, 31
Kurtz, 2, 27
Kurtz, Abraham, 89, 90
Kurtz, Adam, 25, 89
Kurtz, Elizabeth, 100
Kurtz, Fanny, 99, 100
Kurtz, Hans, 90, 107
Kurtz, Jacob, 16, 25, 89, 90
Kurtz, Jakob, 89
Kurtz, Joseph, 100
Kurtz, Stephen, 90

— L —

Landis, Edwin P., 113
Landis, Elwood, 113
Lantz, 2
Lantz, Hans, 14
Laymon, Mary, 98
Lefever, Paul, 16
Lehman, Anna, 85
Lehman, Benedict, 3, 4, 5, 11, 22, 27, 33, 57, 77, 90, 113, 117
Lehman, Benedict, Jr., 2, 3, 11
Lehman, Benedict, Sr., 2, 3
Lehman, David, 109
Lehman, Elizabeth, 97
Lehman, Ferona, 2
Lehman, Isaac, 54
Lehman, John, 54, 113
Lehman, Magdalena, 33, 57, 119
Lehman, Mary, 54
Lehman, Owen, 52, 53
Lehman, Pence, 3
Lehman, Peter, 113
Leibengut, Miss, 101
Leman, Benedict, 90, 113
Leman, John, 113
Lewis, Catherine, 62
Lewis, Esther, 62
Lichty, Miss, 101
Lint family, 30
Lint, Catherine, 30
Lint, Jacob, 30
Livengood family, 30
Livengood, Catherine, 49, 98
Livengood, Christian, 6, 7
Livengood, Elizabeth, 48, 49
Livengood, Mary, 49
Livengood, Peter, 3, 4, 6, 7, 9, 45, 49, 58, 98
Livingston, Anna, 79
Livingston, Barbara, 79
Livingston, David, 78, 79, 81
Long, ___, 48

— M —

Mast, 2, 4
Mast, Abraham, 99, 100
Mast, Catherine, 99, 100
Mast, Elizabeth, 98, 99, 100
Mast, Fanny, 99, 100
Mast, Jacob, 1, 12, 13, 14, 17, 102

Mast, Jacob, Bish., 108
Mast, Joseph, 45, 49, 96, 101, 102
Mast, Mary, 99, 100, 102
Mast, Noah, 98
Mast, Rebecca, 100
Mast, Sarah, 45, 49, 96, 100, 101
Mast, Susanna, 100, 101
Mast, Susannah, 101
Mast, Veronica, 100
Maurer, Johannes, 89
Maust, Fern Glessner, 113
Maust, Jacob, Bish., 108
Maust, Lewis, 107
Maust, Lewis, Mr./Mrs., 107
Maust, Thomas, 7, 20, 119
Maust, Thomas, Jr., 22, 70
Maust, Thomas, Sr., 20, 22
Maust, Thomas, Sr., Mr./Mrs., 118
Maust, Thomas Irvin, II, 105
Maust, Tom, 108, 117
Maust, Tom, Jr., 117, 118
McSummy, William, 67
Menges, Barbara, 62
Menges, John, 62
Meyers family, 29, 30
Meyers, Catherine, 71
Miller, 29
Miller, Aaron, 99
Miller, Aaron T., 99
Miller, Abraham, 2, 11, 16, 17, 19, 34, 45, 46, 49, 62, 86, 90, 101, 109, 115
Miller, Absalom, 97
Miller, Adam, 97
Miller, Alvin J., 93
Miller, Amelia, 98
Miller, Andrew, 100
Miller, Anna, 8, 36, 39, 40, 41, 42, 45, 49, 59, 60, 62, 63, 66, 91, 96, 98, 100, 101, 102
Miller, Annas, 98
Miller, Annie, 101
Miller, Barbara, 2, 4, 6, 7, 8, 9, 11, 14, 19, 28, 29, 43, 44, 46, 49, 58, 60, 62, 65, 66, 67, 68, 73, 91, 93, 96, 97, 98, 99, 100, 101, 102
Miller, Benedick, 98
Miller, Benedict, ix, 40, 43, 44, 49, 91, 93, 96, 97, 98, 115
Miller, Benjamin, 38, 99, 100
Miller, Benjamin D., 95
Miller, Benjamin J., 95
Miller, Catherine, vii, 7, 35, 42, 43, 45, 49, 51, 53,

54, 55, 56, 59, 60, 62, 80, 91, 96, 97, 98, 100, 101, 102, 103
Miller, Catherine J., 100, 105
Miller, Christian, vii, 2, 7, 9, 11, 14, 20, 22, 51, 55, 57, 58, 59, 60, 61, 65, 66, 69, 73, 77, 86, 90, 96, 99, 101, 108, 115, 117, 118
Miller, Christian, Jr., 16
Miller, Christian, Sr., 16
Miller, Christian Glades, 62
Miller, Christian "Schmidt," Bish., 55, 66
Miller, Corey, 48
Miller, Corrie, 48
Miller, Crippled John, 22
Miller, Daniel, 35, 68, 70, 86, 93, 98, 99, 100, 101, 102
Miller, Daniel B., 19, 38, 95
Miller, Daniel S., 67, 68
Miller, Darrell, 41
Miller, David, 17, 20, 34, 35, 62, 91, 93, 98, 99, 100, 102
Miller, Dinah, 101, 102
Miller, Dorothea, 98
Miller, Eli, 98
Miller, Eli D., 100
Miller, Elias, 36, 99, 102
Miller, Eliza, 102
Miller, Elizabeth, 35, 36, 48, 49, 62, 66, 67, 68, 82, 84, 93, 97, 98, 99, 100, 101, 102
Miller, Emanuel, 36, 99, 100, 101
Miller, Enoch, 97
Miller, Ephraim, 102
Miller, Ernest, 48
Miller, Esther, 62
Miller, Eva, 98, 100
Miller, Evan, ix
Miller, Fanny, 99, 100
Miller, Frany, 102
Miller, Freny, 7, 8, 16, 33, 34, 35, 57, 59, 60, 61, 63, 68, 73, 74, 75, 77, 86, 93
Miller, Gertraut, 99
Miller, Gertrude, 98
Miller, Glades Christian, 57, 59, 60, 61, 108
Miller, Glee Mose, 49, 91, 104
Miller, Gross Mose, 91, 94, 102, 104
Miller, Hannes, v, 1, 2, 3, 4, 5, 7, 9, 11, 14, 15, 22, 61, 62, 77, 90, 116
Miller, Hannes, Jr., 7, 9, 10, 33
Miller, Hannes, Sr., 34, 108, 113
Miller, Hans, v
Miller, Henry, 40, 43, 44, 62, 66, 91, 96, 97, 98, 100, 101
Miller, Howard, 48
Miller, Indian John, 22, 108
Miller, Isaac, 36, 62, 82, 83, 84, 86, 98, 99, 101, 102
Miller, Isaac D., 100
Miller, Isaac H., 101
Miller, Ivan J., 93
Miller, J. Virgil, viii, ix, 28, 32, 36, 38, 40, 41, 48, 52, 53, 104, 116, 119
Miller, Jacob, 1, 2, 5, 7, 8, 9, 11, 12, 13, 16, 17, 19, 20, 27, 33, 34, 35, 39, 40, 41, 42, 43, 45, 57, 58, 60, 61, 69, 75, 82, 90, 91, 93, 96, 98, 99, 100, 101, 102, 103, 107, 108, 109
Miller, Jacob, Bish., 96, 106
Miller, Jacob, Jr., 40, 41, 43, 44, 85
Miller, Jacob, Sr., 85
Miller, Jacob B., 97
Miller, Jacob D., 97
Miller, Jacob J., 62
Miller, James A., 104
Miller, James Virgil, 95
Miller, Jay, 97
Miller, Jeremiah, 48, 49, 101
Miller, Jeremiah, Jr., 48, 49
Miller, Joel, 97, 98
Miller, Joel B., 43, 93
Miller, Joel J., 93
Miller, John, v, 3, 4, 6, 7, 14, 16, 17,22, 31, 36, 40, 43, 59, 60, 61, 62, 66, 86, 91, 96, 98, 99, 100, 101, 102, 103, 108, 116, 117
Miller, John, Jr., 5, 6, 7, 8, 9, 17, 19, 20, 27, 33, 34, 35, 36, 37, 45, 46, 58, 61, 91, 95
Miller, John, Sr., i, ix, 2, 5, 7, 9, 10, 11, 16, 17, 18, 19, 20, 21, 22, 23, 25, 27, 29, 33, 35, 39, 40, 45, 51, 57, 58, 65, 69, 73, 75, 78, 82, 83, 84, 86, 91, 93, 95, 118, 119
Miller, John (Broad Run), 49
Miller, John A., 47
Miller, John J., 42, 43, 97, 98
Miller, John S., 68, 103
Miller, Jonas, 45, 49, 91, 93, 96, 100, 101, 102, 103
Miller, Jonas B., 93
Miller, Jonathan, 55, 68, 99, 101, 102
Miller, Joni, 55
Miller, Joseph, 7, 9, 47, 48, 49, 51, 54, 58, 59, 60, 62, 64, 65, 66, 67, 68, 69, 73, 74, 82, 93, 96, 98, 99, 101, 102, 115
Miller, Joseph, Pre., 68
Miller, Joseph J., 68
Miller, Jost, 66
Miller, Judith, 98, 100
Miller, Keim Christian, 59
Miller, Klein Mose, 49, 91, 104
Miller, Leah, 99, 100
Miller, Levi, 98
Miller, Lucy, 98, 102
Miller, Lydia, 68, 98, 99, 102
Miller, Magdalena, 3, 5, 9, 10, 22, 33, 35, 45, 48, 49, 55, 56, 57, 62, 63, 66, 69, 91, 96, 98, 99, 100, 101, 102, 108, 119
Miller, Mahlon, 102
Miller, Manassas, 98
Miller, Margaret, 68, 103
Miller, Maria, 7, 69, 70, 71, 99, 102
Miller, Marie, ix, 35, 38
Miller, Mary, 7, 8, 34, 36, 45, 47, 48, 49, 59, 62, 66, 97, 98, 99, 100, 101, 102
Miller, Michael, 3, 20, 99, 100
Miller, Mill, 99
Miller, Moses, 45, 49, 91, 94, 99, 100, 101, 102, 103. 104
Miller, Moses B., vii, 1, 19, 96, 97
Miller, Moses J., 49, 91, 100, 104
Miller, Moses P., 49, 91
Miller, Moses T., 99
Miller, Nancy, 99, 102
Miller, Nicholas, 2, 3, 4, 5, 14, 16, 20, 25, 27, 57, 69, 73, 84, 86, 113, 117
Miller, Nicholas, Sr., 27
Miller, Noah, 100
Miller, Peter, 5, 7, 8, 9, 16, 19, 29, 31, 33, 34, 39, 45, 46, 47, 48, 49, 54, 58, 59, 60, 62, 91, 96, 97, 98, 101, 102
Miller, Peter, Jr., 47, 48
Miller, Peter G., 62
Miller, Peter J., 94
Miller, Peter P., 45, 46, 47, 48,

123

49, 101
Miller, Philipine, 102
Miller, Phoebe F., 97
Miller, Polly, 68, 101
Miller, Rachel, 42, 68
Miller, Rachel A., 100
Miller, Rebecca, 66, 97, 98, 99, 100
Miller, Sally, 98, 101, 102
Miller, Saloma, 97
Miller, Samuel, 16, 68
Miller, Samuel J., 47
Miller, Samuel P., 47, 48, 102
Miller, Samuel S., 48
Miller, Sarah, 36, 45, 48, 49, 67, 91, 96, 97, 99, 101, 102
Miller, Schmidt Christian, 59
Miller, Shem, 100, 101
Miller, Sim, 98
Miller, Simon, 100, 101
Miller, Solomon, 36, 58, 59, 60, 63, 97, 98, 99, 100, 101, 103
Miller, Stephen, 99, 100
Miller, Susan, ix, 99, 102
Miller, Susanna, 7, 48, 77, 78, 79, 97, 99, 100, 101, 102
Miller, Susannah, 98, 101
Miller, Tobias, 99
Miller, Ura R., 95
Miller, Vernon D., 94
Miller, Veronica, 7, 86, 98, 100, 102
Miller, William, 101
Miller, Wounded John, 22
Miller, Yockel, 34, 40
Miller, Yost, 17, 19, 20, 34, 35, 37, 38, 91, 92, 93, 95, 97, 98, 99, 100, 101, 102
Miller, Yost B., 92
Miller, Zachariah, 98
Miltenberger, John, 55
Miltenberger, Rachel, 55, 59, 63
Mischle, Josep, 90
Mischler, Hans, 89
Mischler, Ulrich, 89, 90
Mishler, 2, 110
Mishler, Anna, 79
Mishler, Barbara, 79, 80, 100
Mishler, Catherine, 80, 103
Mishler, Christian, 7, 77, 78, 79, 80, 81, 85, 103
Mishler, Christian, Jr., 79
Mishler, Christian, Mrs., 96, 103, 108
Mishler, Christina, 74, 77
Mishler, Daniel, 80

Mishler, David, 80
Mishler, Elizabeth, 79, 103
Mishler, Freny, 16, 77
Mishler, Gabriel, 79
Mishler, Jacob, 77, 78, 79, 81
Mishler, Jacob D., 80
Mishler, John, 79
Mishler, Jonas, 80, 103
Mishler, Joseph, 74, 77, 78, 79, 113
Mishler, Levi, 79
Mishler, Lydia, 80
Mishler, Magdalena, 80, 100
Mishler, Peter, 80
Mishler, Susan, 79
Mishler, Susanna, 7, 77, 78, 79, 80, 85
Mishler, Tobias, 79, 80, 103
Misseler, Jacob, 90
Mittenbeger, John, 53
Mosser, Mary, 36
Mosser, Polly, 101
Müller, Anna, 26
Müller, Barbara, 24, 26
Müller, Catharina, 26
Müller, Christen, 24
Müller, Christian, 26, 89
Müller, Claus, 25, 89
Müller, Daniel, 24
Müller, Elisabetha, 25
Müller, Elsbeth, 24
Müller, Hainest, 23
Müller, Hans, 24
Müller, Heini, 23, 24
Müller, Heinrich, 24
Müller, Henry, 23, 24, 87
Müller, Jacob, 25, 26, 27
Müller, Jakob, 25, 26, 89
Müller, Johann, 25, 26, 89
Müller, Johannes, v, 23, 24, 26, 27
Müller, Mädli, 24
Müller, Magdalena, 26
Müller, Michael, 25, 89
Müller, Nicolaus, 25
Müller, Nikel, 25
Mullet, Benedict, 100
Mullet, Eva, 100
Musser, Rebecca, 85

— N —

Nafzger, Mattheis, 90
Nafziger, 2, 27
Nafziger, Barbara, 26
Nafziger, Johannes, 26, 89
Newcomer, Christian, 74
Newcomer, Rev., 74, 75
Nissli, Christian, 115
— O —

Oesch, Jacob, 115
Olds, Miss, 98

— P —

Phennicle, Frank, 113
Plank, Lydia, 56
Plank, Rebecca, 55, 56
Platt, Clyde L., 113
Platt, Ruth, 113
Plough, Christian, 106

— Q —

Qnäg, Johannes, 90

— R —

Ramsberger, Juliana, 71
Reber, Philipine, 102
Richardson, Elizabeth, 97
Riley, Martin, 59
Ringenberg, Hans, 89
Robinson, Hugh, 29, 45, 46
Rogy, Barbara, 26
Rupp, Hans, 89

— S —

Sala, John, 63
Sala, Magdalena, 63
Saylor, 29
Saylor, E. C., Dr., 109
Saylor, Jacob, 34
Saylor, John, 3, 34
Saylor, Mary, 34, 49
Saylor, Sally, 101
Schambrick, Anna, 98
Schantz, 110
Schantz, Joseph, 107
Schlatter, Anna, 49
Schmucker, Mary, 101
Schrack, John, 106
Schrag, Casper, 69, 70, 89, 117
Schrag, Johannes, 69, 90
Schrag, John, 69, 106
Schrag, John, Mrs., 96
Schrag, Maria, 70
Schrag, Peter, 99
Schrag, Sarah, 99
Schrag, Uli, 70
Schrag, Ulrich, 70, 89
Schritchfield, Mrs., 97
Schrock, Aaron, 71
Schrock, Alta, Dr., 47, 93
Schrock, Anna, 102
Schrock, Barbara, 71, 97
Schrock, Benjamin, 102
Schrock, Caroline, 71

Schrock, Casper, 69, 70, 113
Schrock, Catherine, 71, 102
Schrock, Christian, 70, 71
Schrock, Daniel, 71
Schrock, Dorothea, 71
Schrock, Elizabeth, 70, 71
Schrock, Fanny, 71
Schrock, Frantz, 71
Schrock, Gertrude, 71
Schrock, J. B., 109
Schrock, Jacob, 71, 113
Schrock, Jacob B., 109
Schrock, James J., 71
Schrock, Johannes, 69
Schrock, John, 69, 71, 82, 83, 106, 111, 117
Schrock, John, Mrs., 108
Schrock, John, Jr., 7, 69, 70, 71
Schrock, John, Sr., 70
Schrock, Joseph, 71
Schrock, Lydia, 102
Schrock, Magdalena, 71, 102
Schrock, Margaret, 71
Schrock, Maria, 7, 69, 70, 71, 82
Schrock, Mary, 7, 70, 71
Schrock, Michael, 71, 109
Schrock, Rosanne, 71
Schrock, Samuel, 71
Schrock, Susanna, 71, 102
Schrock, Uli, 70
Schrock, Ulrich, 70
Schrock, Yost, 71, 72
Schryack, John, 106
Schultz family, 30
Schultz, Mary, 30, 32
Schwartzendruber, 110
Schwartzendruber, Jacob, 109
Schwarzendrover, Elizabeth, 48
Seese, Barbara, 43, 44
Seese, George, 44
Seicher, Jonathan, 84
Seiler, 2
Seiler, Jacob, 34
Seiler, John, 34
Shanover, Eva, 98
Shanover, Jacob, 98
Shaulis, Anna, 75
Shaulis, John, 75
Ship-*Amish Mayflower*, 11
Ship-*Brotherhood*, 2
Ship-*Charming Nancy*, 2, 11, 14, 16, 73, 82, 90
Ship-*Frances & Elizabeth*, 90
Ship-*Muscliffe Galley*, 90
Ship-*Phoenix*, 1, 77, 90
Ship-*Polly*, 90
Ship-*Sally*, 90
Shrake, John, 106

Shultz, John W., 113
Shultz, Vera, 113
Siler, John, 3
Skilling, Mill, 99
Slabaugh, John Mark, 17
Slagle, Henry, 31
Slagle, Katherine, 31
Slagle, Mollie, 31
Smiley, George, 59
Smiley, John, 66
Smiley, Nathan, 66
Smiley, Rebecca, 66
Snavely, 62
Sommers, Barbara, 102
Sommers, Elizabeth, 99, 102
Sommers, Joseph, 102
Speicher family, 2, 69
Speicher, Abraham, 85
Speicher, Anna, 73, 85
Speicher, Barbara,7, 58, 65, 66, 73, 82, 93
Speicher, Christian, 3, 4, 5, 20, 58, 65, 70, 84, 113, 117
Speicher, Christian, Mrs., 96, 108
Speicher, Christian, Jr., 7, 73, 74, 75, 82, 93, 117
Speicher, Christian, Sr., 7, 73, 74, 77, 82, 93
Speicher, Christina, 74, 77
Speicher, David, 76
Speicher, Dinah, 102
Speicher, Elizabeth, 75, 82, 83, 84, 85, 93
Speicher, Fanny, 99
Speicher, Freny, 7, 73, 74, 75, 93
Speicher, Henry, 84
Speicher, Huldah, 84
Speicher, Jacob, 84
Speicher, John, 73, 74, 102
Speicher, Jonathan, 76
Speicher, Joseph, 9, 10, 73, 74, 75, 82, 83, 84, 85, 86, 93, 117
Speicher, Joseph, Mrs., 96, 108
Speicher, Joseph, Jr., 74, 85
Speicher, Joseph, Sr., 74
Speicher, Mary, 85
Speicher, Rebecca, 85
Speicher, Samuel, 73, 74
Speicher, Sarah, 85
Speicher, Solomon, 85
Speicher, Susanna, 85
Speicher, Tobias, 85
Speicher, Ulrich, 15, 73, 82, 90
Speicher, Veronica, 7
Spelcher, Christian, 107
Spiker, Abraham, 75
Spiker, Anna, 75

Spiker, Catherine, 75
Spiker, Christian, 3, 74, 113
Spiker, David, 75, 76
Spiker, Elizabeth, 75
Spiker, Jacob, 85
Spiker, Jacob C., 75
Spiker, John, 74
Spiker, Jonathan, 75, 76
Spiker, Magdalena, 75
Spiker, Margaret, 75
Spiker, Rachel, 75
Stehley, Barbara, 14
Stehley, Christian, 14
Stehley, Henry, 14
Stehley, Ulrich, 14
Stevanus, Elizabeth, 30, 32
Stoltzfus, Christian, 90
Stoltzfus, Nicholas, 89
Stoltzfus, Nikel, 90
Stuckey, Maria, 70
Stutzman, Anna, 8, 33, 39, 42, 45, 73, 96
Stutzman, Barbara, 8, 33, 39, 45, 102
Stutzman, Christian, 8, 33
Stutzman, Elizabeth, 100
Stutzman, Jacob, 33, 102
Stutzman, John, 73, 74
Stutzman, Jonas, 96
Stutzman, Magdalena, 33, 102
Stutzman, Mary, 8, 45, 48, 49
Stutzman, Sally, 102
Stutzman, Sarah, 101
Suder, James I., 113
Suder, Norman E., 113
Summers, Elizabeth, 98
Summers, Joseph, 98
Sutter, Margaret, 68, 103
Swartzendruber, David, 102
Swartzendruber, Jacob, 110, 115
Swartzendruber, Mary, 102
Sweet, George, 44

— T —

Talmadge, Phoebe F., 97
Thomas, Anna, 63
Thomas, Catherine, 63
Thomas, Freny, 59, 60, 63
Thomas, Jacob, 55, 59, 60, 63
Thomas, Jakob, 55
Thomas, John, 55
Thomas, John, Mrs., 103
Thomas, Magdalena, 80
Thomas, Maria, 55
Thomas, Peter, 63
Thomas, Rachel, 55, 59, 60, 63
Troyer, 110
Troyer, Elizabeth, 35, 100

Troyer, Freny, 35
Troyer, Hans, 98
Troyer, John, 45, 49, 54, 96, 101, 113
Troyer, Lydia, 98
Troyer, Magdalena, 35, 45, 49, 96, 99, 101
Troyer, Michael, 3, 113
Troyer, Michael, Jr., 70
Troyer, Sally, 98
Troyer, Sarah, 99
Troyer, Veronica, 100

— V —

Vought, Bertha S., 113
Vought, Merl, 113

— W —

Walker family, 31
Walker, Earl L., 113
Weaver, Abraham, 101
Weaver, Barbara, 101
Weaver, Catherine, 100
Weaver, David, 80
Weaver, David, Mrs., 103
Weaver, Dinah, 101
Weaver, Freny, 66
Weaver, John, 80
Weaver, Jonas, 66
Weaver, Magdalena, 80, 100
Weaver, Peter S., 100
Weaver, Susanna, 80, 101
Weaver, William, 101
Weibel, Levi, 97
Weibel, Rebecca, 97
Weiler, Elizabeth, 75
Weirich, Philip, 67, 102
Weirich, Sarah, 67, 102
Welti, Christian, 98
Welti, Dorothea, 98
Wenger, Leah, 99
Wenger, Lydia, 99
Wengerd, 62

Wertz, Barbara, 102
Wertz, Daniel, 102
Will, Calvin, 117
Will, Calvin M., 112, 113
Will, Jim, Mr./Mrs., 108
Willard, Catherine, 42, 97
Willard, Henry, 97
Wingard, Catherine, 32
Winger, Catherine, 30
Witwer, Hans, 23

— Y —

Yansey, Anna, 102
Yergin, Catherine, 75
Yoder, 62
Yoder, Abner, 109
Yoder, Adam, 101
Yoder, Amelia, 98
Yoder, Anna, 33
Yoder, Barbara, 34, 49, 98, 101
Yoder, Benedict, 110
Yoder, Benjamin, 71
Yoder, Catherine, 97, 98, 102, 103
Yoder, Christian, 33, 34, 55, 56, 58, 83, 90, 102, 113
Yoder, Christian, Jr., 109, 115
Yoder, Christian, Sr., 108, 109, 115
Yoder, Daniel, 103
Yoder, David, 109, 113, 115
Yoder, Eliza, 102
Yoder, Elizabeth, 36, 62, 68, 71, 85, 98, 99, 101, 102
Yoder, Emanuel, 62
Yoder, Fanny, 100
Yoder, Freny, 8, 33, 34, 35, 55, 56
Yoder, Gertraut, 34, 35, 99
Yoder, Gertrude, 55, 71
Yoder, Isaac, 79, 85
Yoder, Jacob, 33, 34, 35, 37, 90, 98, 100, 101
Yoder, Jacob D., 98

Yoder, Jacob S., 98
Yoder, John, 33, 34, 37, 98, 100, 113
Yoder, Jonas, 115
Yoder, Joseph, 85, 102
Yoder, Joseph J., 71
Yoder, Joseph S., 102
Yoder, Jost, 115
Yoder, Judith, 55
Yoder, Juliana, 71
Yoder, Lucy, 98
Yoder, Magdalena, 33, 98
Yoder, Marie, ix
Yoder, Mary, 36, 98, 101
Yoder, Moses D., 98
Yoder, Paul, ix
Yoder, Peter, 55
Yoder, Sarah, 85
Yoder, Schweitzer, 108
Yoder, Stephen, 85, 98
Yoder, Susan, 79, 99
Yoder, Susanna, 85
Yoder, Tobias W., 85
Yoder, Veronica, 71, 98
Yoder, Yost, 6, 34
Yutzy, George, 62
Yutzy, Mary, 100

— Z —

Zook, 110
Zook, Christian, 108
Zook, Fanny, 99
Zoug, Christen, 89
Zuck, Christian, 3
Zuck, Yost, 3
Zug, 110
Zug, Christian, 3, 6, 16, 77, 90, 108, 113
Zug, Jacob, 110
Zug, Johannes, 16, 90
Zug, John, 113
Zug, Moritz, 16, 90
Zug, Yost, 3, 4